"Magical. . . . If you read this book patiently and honestly, it may begin to change your attitude and thought process. Deeply and impressively subversive in more ways than one, this book invites us directly in the search for meaning of our work and life."
—Ping Fu, Author of *Bend, Not Break: A Life in Two Worlds*, Founder and Former CEO, Geomagic, Inc.

"Not averse to giving 'recipes,' Pattakos makes them transparent and convincing enough, and he amply supports them by personal observations and experiences, by testimonies and quotations, by anecdotes and proven wisdom, adding more than a sprinkle of wit and common sense. And he does it all in an immensely readable style."
—Franz J. Vesely, PhD, Viktor Frankl Institute, Vienna, Austria

"Logotherapy was tested in Nazi concentration camps, so it speaks uniquely of meaning in extremes of unavoidable suffering. But Frankl also encouraged the discovery of meaning in our everyday workplaces, and Pattakos offers both a *why* and a *how*."
—Haddon Klingberg Jr., PhD, Author of *When Life Calls Out to Us: The Love and Lifework of Viktor and Elly Frankl*

"If you want to bring life to your personal and/or organizational values—read *Prisoners of Our Thoughts*. It is particularly helpful if you are committed to living an authentic (values-driven) life. This is a book you will want all your associates and family members to read again and again."
—Ann Rhoades, President, People Ink, and Former Executive Vice President, People, JetBlue Airways

"The transcendent spirit of Viktor Frankl vindicated human resilience. Alex Pattakos nimbly brings essential new life to that spirit. Reading this book is a choice—a choice to add deeper meaning to your life."
—Jeffrey K. Zeig, PhD, Founder and Director, The Milton H. Erickson Foundation

"Living and working in such changing times takes courage. This book helps us connect with ourselves and meaning in order to be happier, develop resilience in life and work, and co-create a better future. In a time when there is so much unpredictability, *Prisoners of Our Thoughts* is a must-read to serve as a prescription for personal and business leadership."
—Lisa Schilling, RN, MPH, Vice President, Healthcare Performance Improvement, Kaiser Permanente

"It is very rare to encounter a book that is simultaneously profound and approachable, one that addresses the essential crux of the human dilemma in a manner that is inviting and even heartfelt. *Prisoners of Our Thoughts* is just such a book. I highly recommend it."
—Jeffrey Mishlove, PhD, Dean of Transformational Psychology, University of Philosophical Research, and Author of *The Roots of Consciousness*

"A must-read for all those who want to lead successful lives. . . . The book has universal appeal and would help people working in any part of the world, and at any type of job. Dr. Pattakos's concepts resonate well with me—a Sikh by religion. I believe that world peace would be greatly helped by having more and more people happy with their lives, as *Prisoners of Our Thoughts* could help them be."
>   —Karuna Singh, Program Manager, Office of Public Affairs, U.S. Consulate General, Kolkata, India

"*Prisoners of Our Thoughts* is an enormously inspiring eye and heart opener, enlarging the scope of our life and work in a wonderful way. It's a book full of wisdom, a road sign to the meaning and riches of life."
>   —Dr. Heinrich Anker, Cofounder, Management Centre Zug (Switzerland), and President, Swiss Society of Logotherapy and Existential Analysis

"CEOs, as well as the average worker, can be both informed and inspired by Pattakos's book."
>   —Paul T. P. Wong, PhD, President, International Network on Personal Meaning, and Coeditor of *The Human Quest for Meaning: A Handbook of Psychological Research and Clinical Applications*

"It has been a long wait—a very long wait! But Frankl's principles and methods have at last been set free to be used and enjoyed and practiced in the work situation."
>   —Dr. Patti Havenga Coetzer, Founder, Viktor Frankl Foundation of South Africa

"Masterpiece. Challenging. Insightful. Motivational. Inspirational. Magnificent. *Prisoners of Our Thoughts* branches all of these into one central theme: staying true to you, the real you. This book is a must-read for all educators, parents, and students. It provides such a clear view of the importance of character and how love ties it all together. A must-read."
>   —Dr. Mark Isley, Principal, Shelby County Alternative School, Alabama

"Those who seek meaning in their work and life will find much of value in this practical application of the wisdom of Dr. Frankl, so deeply experienced and artfully presented."
>   —Dee Hock, Founder and CEO Emeritus, VISA

"Don't let life just happen to you! Let Dr. Pattakos show you how to apply Viktor Frankl's core principles to make your work—and life—more meaningful. Anyone from mail deliverer to CEO can embark on a path of self-discovery that will lead to better results and relationships with others."
>   —Jean E. Spence, Executive Vice President, Global Technology and Quality, Kraft Foods

"I fully recommend reading this great work and applying its wisdom. Please don't wait to open your 'lockbox' of talents and tasks that life has set aside for you. Seek what is yours on behalf of all mankind."
>   —Robert R. Thompson, Lieutenant Colonel, U.S. Army

"Use *Prisoners of Our Thoughts* as a textbook, order it for all your employees, and buy a copy for yourself."

> —Erik Bergrud, Associate Vice President for Alumni, Constituent and Employer Relations, Park University, and Past President, American Society for Public Administration

"Dr. Pattakos provides a commonsense model to resolve the existential anxiety created by the gap between our thoughts and reality and to tremendously enrich our lives. Read *Prisoners of Our Thoughts* and be prepared to look in the mirror and see the person responsible for your dissatisfaction and unhappiness!"

> —Vann E. Schaffner, MD, Spokane, Washington

"Every thinking person can benefit from the work of Alex Pattakos. As we wind our way through life's challenges, understanding life's choices and outcomes is foremost. This work adds a great deal of value to this most important of life's searches."

> —Robert Agranoff, PhD, Professor Emeritus, School of Public and Environmental Affairs, Indiana University, Bloomington

"*Prisoners of Our Thoughts* is a must-read. Not only is it written in very direct, clear language to assert the case for each of us to follow the meaning in our lives, but it hits an intuitive nerve as Dr. Pattakos explains Viktor Frankl's sources for authentic meaning in one's life. This has been a major influence in creating a more rewarding life for me and countless others."

> —Michael E. Skaggs, Executive Director, Nevada Commission on Economic Development

"Alex Pattakos does a wonderful job of translating Frankl's work into actions for living. He delivers an especially powerful message for individuals striving to grow both professionally and personally. I can think of no other book that better prepares leaders for facing tough challenges. This is a must-read for leaders!"

> —Dr. Mitch Owen, College of Agriculture and Life Sciences, North Carolina State University

Viktor Frankl's Principles
for Discovering Meaning in Life and Work

PRISONERS OF OUR THOUGHTS

THIRD EDITION, REVISED AND EXPANDED

ALEX PATTAKOS, PhD

ELAINE DUNDON

Berrett–Koehler Publishers, Inc.
a BK Life book

Berrett-Koehler Publishers, Inc.
1333 Broadway, Suite 1000
Oakland, CA 94612 USA
Tel: (510) 817-2277; Fax: (510) 817-2278; www.bkconnection.com

Ordering Information

Quantity sales. Special discounts are available on quantity purchases by corporations, associations, and others. For details, contact the "Special Sales Department" at the Berrett-Koehler address above.

Individual sales. Berrett-Koehler publications are available through most bookstores. They can also be ordered direct from Berrett-Koehler: Tel: (800) 929-2929; Fax: (802) 864-7626; www.bkconnection.com

Orders for college textbook/course adoption use. Please contact Berrett-Koehler: Tel: (800) 929-2929; Fax: (802) 864-7626.

Orders by U.S. trade bookstores and wholesalers. Please contact Ingram Publisher Services: Tel: (800) 509-4887; Fax: (800) 838-1149; Email: customer.service@ingram publisherservices.com; or visit www.ingrampublisherservices.com/Ordering for details about electronic ordering.

Berrett-Koehler and the BK logo are registered trademarks of Berrett-Koehler Publishers, Inc.

Printed in the United States of America

Berrett-Koehler books are printed on long-lasting acid-free paper. When it is available, we choose paper that has been manufactured by environmentally responsible processes. These may include using trees grown in sustainable forests, incorporating recycled paper, minimizing chlorine in bleaching, or recycling the energy produced at the paper mill.

Library of Congress Cataloging-in-Publication Data

Pattakos, Alex, author. | Dundon, Elaine, 1959– author.
    Prisoners of our thoughts : Viktor Frankl's principles for discovering meaning in life and work / Alex Pattakos, PhD, & Elaine Dundon.
    Third edition, revised and expanded. | Oakland : Berrett-Koehler Publishers, Inc., a BK Life book, [2017] | Includes bibliographical references and index.
    LCCN 2016029733 | ISBN 9781626568808 (pbk.)
    Subjects: LCSH: Frankl, Viktor E. (Viktor Emil), 1905–1997. | Logotherapy. | Meaning (Psychology) | Conduct of life.
    LCC RC440.5.P38 2017 | DDC 616.89/14—dc23 LC record available at https://lccn.loc.gov/2016029733
    Third edition

21 20 19 18 17 16 | 10 9 8 7 6 5 4 3 2 1

Project management: BookMatters; copyediting by Amy Smith Bell; proofreading by Janet Reed Blake; index by Leonard Rosenbaum; text design by Detta Penna; typesetting by BookMatters; cover design by Barbara Haines; cover image © iStockphoto.com/Sascha Burkard

This book is dedicated to

Viktor E. Frankl, MD, PhD (1905–1997)
and
Dr. Stephen R. Covey (1932–2012)

whose lives and legacies will forever bring light
to darkness, as well as to all the people around
the world who are searching for meaning.

Contents

Applying the therapeutic system of world-renowned psychiatrist and existential philosopher Viktor E. Frankl, learn how to bring personal meaning and fulfillment to your everyday life and work and achieve your highest potential!

Core Principles

❶ *Exercise the freedom to choose your attitude.* In all situations, no matter how desperate they may appear or actually be, you always have the ultimate freedom to choose your attitude.

❷ *Realize your will to meaning.* Commit authentically to meaningful values and goals that only you can actualize and fulfill.

❸ *Detect the meaning of life's moments.* Only you can answer for your own life by detecting the meaning at any given moment and assuming responsibility for weaving your unique tapestry of existence.

❹ *Don't work against yourself.* Avoid becoming so fixated on an intent or outcome that you actually work against the desired result.

❺ *Look at yourself from a distance.* Only human beings possess the capacity to look at themselves from a distance, with a sense of perspective, including the uniquely human trait known as your sense of humor.

❻ *Shift your focus of attention.* Deflect your attention from the problem situation to something else and build your coping mechanisms for dealing with stress and change.

❼ *Extend beyond yourself.* Manifest the human spirit at work by directing your attention and relating to something more than yourself.

Foreword

Shortly before Viktor Frankl's passing in September 1997, I had heard of his declining health, illness, and hospitalization. I was very anxious to talk with him so that I could express my profound gratitude for his life's work—for his impact on millions of people, including my own life and life's work. I understood that he had lost his sight and that his wife was reading to him several hours each day in the hospital. I will never forget the feeling of hearing his voice and visiting with him. He was so kind and gracious as he listened to my expressions of appreciation, esteem, and love. I felt as if I were speaking to a great and noble spirit. After patiently listening, he said, "Stephen, you talk to me as if I am ready to check out. I still have two important projects I need to complete." How true to form! How true to character! How true to the principles of Logotherapy!

Frankl's desire and determination to continue to contribute reminded me of his collaborative work with Dr. Hans Selye of Montreal, Canada—famous for his research and writings on stress. Selye taught that it is only when we have meaningful work and projects that our immune system is strengthened and the degenerative aging forces are slowed down. He called this kind of stress "eustress" rather than distress, which comes from a life without meaning and integrity. I'm sure these two souls influenced each other, reinforcing both the physical and psychological benefits of Logotherapy, of man's search for meaning.

When Alex Pattakos graciously invited me to write a foreword to *Prisoners of Our Thoughts* and told me that the Frankl family had suggested this to him, I was both honored and excited to participate—particularly since they felt my work with organizations in management and leadership beautifully paralleled Viktor Frankl's "principles at work," the heart of this splendid book. My sense of the significance of this book deepened further when Pattakos wrote me, "A year before he died, I was sitting with Dr. Frankl in his study and he grabbed my arm and said, 'Alex, yours is the book that needs to be written!'"

I will never forget how deeply moved and inspired I was in the sixties when I studied *Man's Search for Meaning* and also *The Doctor and the Soul*. These two books, along with Frankl's other writings and lectures, reaffirmed my "soul's code" regarding our power of choice, our unique endowment of self-awareness, and our essence, our will for meaning. While on a writing sabbatical in Hawaii and in a very reflective state of mind, I was wandering through the stacks of a university library and picked up a book. I read the following three lines, which literally staggered me and again reaffirmed Frankl's essential teachings:

> Between stimulus and response, there is a space.
> In that space lies our freedom and our power to choose our
>   response.
> In our response lies our growth and our happiness.

I did not note the name of the author, so I've never been able to give proper attribution. On a later trip to Hawaii I even went back to find the source and found the library building itself was no longer present.

The space between what happens to us and our response, our freedom to choose that response and the impact it can have upon our lives, beautifully illustrate that we can become a product of our decisions, not our conditions. They illustrate the three values that Frankl continually taught: the creative value, the experiential value, and the attitudinal value. We have the power to choose our response to our circumstances. We have the power to shape our circumstances; indeed, we have the responsibility, and if we ignore this space, this freedom, this responsibility, the essence of our life and our legacy could be frustrated.

One time I was leaving a military base where I had been teaching principle-centered leadership over a period of time. As I was saying good-bye to the commander of that base, a colonel, I asked him, "Why would you undertake such a significant change effort to bring principle-centered living and leadership to your command when you know full well you will be swimming upstream against powerful cultural forces? You are in your thirtieth year and you are retiring at the end of this year. You have had a successful military career and you could simply maintain the successful pattern you've had and go into your retirement with all of the honors and the plaudits that come with your dedicated years of service." His answer was unforgettable. It seared itself into my soul. He said, "Recently, my father passed away. Knowing that he was dying, he called my mother and myself to his bedside. He motioned to me to come close to him so that he could whisper something in my ear. My mother stood by, watching in tears. My father said, 'Son, promise me you won't do life like I did. Son, I didn't do right by you or by your mother, and I never really made a difference. Son, promise me you won't do life like I did.'"

This military commander said, "Stephen, that is why I am undertaking this change effort. That is why I want to bring our whole command to an entirely new level of performance and contribution. I want to make a difference, and for the first time I sincerely hope that my successors do better than I have. Up to this point, I had hoped that I would be the high-water mark, but no longer. I want to get these principles so institutionalized and so built into our culture that they will be sustainable and go on and on. I know it will be a struggle. I may even ask for an extension so that I can continue to see this work through, but I want to honor the greatest legacy that my father ever gave me, and that is the desire to make a difference."

From this commander we learn that courage is not the absence of fear but the awareness there is something more important. We spend at least a third of our life either preparing for work or doing work, usually inside organizations. Even our retirement should be filled with meaningful projects, inside organizations or families or societies. Work and love essentially comprise the essence of mortality.

The great humanistic psychologist Abraham Maslow came to similar thoughts near the end of his life, which essentially affirmed Frankl's "will to meaning" theme. He felt that his own need hierarchy theory was too needs determined and that self-actualization was not the highest need. In the end, he concluded that self-transcendence was the human soul's highest need, which reflected more the spirit of Frankl. Maslow's wife, Bertha, and his research associate put together his final thinking along these lines in the book *The Farther Reaches of Human Nature.*

My own work with organizations and with people in the world of work focuses a great deal on developing personal and organizational mission statements. I have found that when you get enough people interacting freely and synergistically, and when these people are informed about the realities of their industry or profession and their own culture, they begin to tap into a kind of collective conscience and awareness of the need to add value, to really leave a legacy, and they set up value guidelines to fulfill that legacy. Ends and means are inseparable; in fact, the ends preexist in the means. No worthy end can ever really be accomplished with unworthy means.

I have found in my teaching that the single most exhilarating, thrilling, and motivating idea that people have ever really seriously contemplated is the idea of the power of choice—the idea that the best way to predict their future is to create it. It is basically the idea of personal freedom, of learning to ask Viktor Frankl's question: What is life asking of me? What is this situation asking of me? It's more freedom *to* rather than freedom *from*. It's definitely an inside-out rather than an outside-in approach.

I have found that when people get caught up in this awareness, this kind of mindfulness, and if they genuinely ask such questions and consult their conscience, almost always the purposes and values they come up with are transcen-dent—that is, they deal with meaning that is larger than their own life, one that truly adds value and contributes to other people's lives—the kinds of things that Viktor Frankl did in the death camps of Nazi Germany. They break cycles; they establish new cycles, new positive energies. They become what I like to call "transition figures"—people who break with past cultural mindless patterns of behavior and attitude.

> The range of what we see and do
> Is limited by what we fail to notice.
> And because we fail to notice
> That we fail to notice,
> There is little we can do
> To change
> Until we notice
> How failing to notice
> Shapes our thoughts and deeds.
>
> —R. D. Laing

With this kind of thinking and with the seven magnifi-cent principles Dr. Pattakos describes in this important book, a kind of primary greatness is developed where character and contribution, conscience and love, choice and meaning, all have their play and synergy with each other. This is contrast-ed with secondary greatness, being those who are successful in society's eyes but personally unfulfilled.

Finally, let me suggest two ideas on how to get the very most from this book. First, share or teach the core principles, one by one, to those you live with and work around who might be interested. Second, live them. To learn something but not to do is really not to learn. To know something but

not to do is really not to know. Otherwise, if we just intel-
lectualize these core principles and verbalize them but do not
share and practice them, we would be like a person who is
blind from birth explaining to another person what it means
to see, based on an academic study of light, its properties,
the eye and its anatomy. As you read this book, I challenge
you to experience the freedom to choose your own attitude,
to exercise your will to meaning, to detect the meaning of
life's moments, to not work against yourself, to look at yourself from a distance, and to shift your focus of attention and
extend beyond yourself. I suggest you consider learning this
material sequentially, by reading the first principle, teaching
it and applying it, then reading the next one, and so forth.
You may want to simply read the entire book all at once to
give yourself the overview, and then go back and learn the
principles sequentially through your own experiencing. You
will become a change catalyst. You will become a transition
figure. You will stop bad cycles and start good ones. Life will
take on a meaning as you've never known it before. I know
this is so from my own experiences and from working with
countless organizations and individuals in the world of work.

As my grandfather taught me, and as Viktor Frankl
taught me, life is a mission, not a career.

Dr. Stephen R. Covey
Author of *The 7 Habits of Highly Effective People*

Preface

Soon after the initial release of *Prisoners of Our Thoughts* in 2004, a massive earthquake under the Indian Ocean triggered one of the deadliest natural disasters in recorded history, known around the world as the Asian Tsunami. This tsunami killed 230,000 people and left 500,000 people homeless. Indonesia's Aceh province was closest to the epicenter of the quake and was hardest hit by the monster waves.

By chance, *Prisoners of Our Thoughts* found its way into the hands of representatives from the Jakarta-based professional services firm Dunamis Organization Services. The company developed a Volunteers' Readiness Program to prepare individuals for what they would encounter while assisting in Aceh. The goal was to teach the volunteers how to respond quickly and effectively to the vast devastation and suffering they would encounter in the field. They also needed to know how to deal with their own psychological reactions. The program, which used *Prisoners of Our Thoughts* as a training resource, was employed by other organizations, including local government bodies and such nongovernmental organizations as UNESCO and UNICEF. All seven core principles described in this book were viewed as essential knowledge, skills, and attitudes required by the volunteer aid workers participating in the readiness program.

In ways we cannot adequately express, this application of the principles in *Prisoners of Our Thoughts* made the book's publication worthwhile—and yes, meaningful—to us. This was not an illustration of the principles in action that Alex had envisioned when he first conceptualized and wrote the book. Far from it! But since its original publication, we have learned that its application potential is unlimited, extending far beyond the realm of work and the workplace.

Not Just for Disasters

Prisoners of Our Thoughts has applications much closer to the lives of most of us. Are you toiling in a job you don't like? Or perhaps you feel the job is okay, but you are not fulfilled by the work? More broadly, do you wonder if there is more to life than what you are experiencing? Have you felt that bad things just happen to you, that your life is out of your control, and there is nothing you can do about it? If you answered "yes" to any of these questions, you are not alone. It is natural to ask such fundamental questions about the way we live and work. This book, written with you in mind, deals with the human quest for meaning. It is grounded in the philosophy and approach of the world-renowned psychiatrist Viktor Frankl, author of the best-selling *Man's Search for Meaning*, which was named one of the ten most influential books in America by the Library of Congress. Frankl's many ideas about the search for meaning, illustrated by his own experiences and those of his clients/patients, have influenced millions around the world.

Frankl, a survivor of Nazi concentration camps during World War II, is most well known for his belief that no matter what challenges you face in life, you always have the ultimate freedom to choose your attitude and your response to what is happening to you. As a prisoner, many things were taken from Frankl: his wife and family, his identity (replaced with a number), his clothing, his health, and his freedom to come and go. Yet he realized that no matter what was happening around and to him, he still retained the capacity to choose his attitude and, by extension, his response. **Frankl *knew* that he was responsible for finding meaning in his circumstances and, importantly, for not becoming a prisoner of his thoughts.** In essence, choosing not to be a passive victim of his circumstances, he practiced an active approach to finding meaning. Similarly, all of us have the ability to respond to the challenges that come our way by exercising our capacity to find meaning. Fundamentally, Frankl believed that there is meaning in every moment of our lives—up to our very last breath—and that it is our personal responsibility to find it. He also underscored that we do not have to suffer in order to find or experience meaning.

Frankl is the founder of Logotherapy, a meaning-centered, humanistic approach to psychotherapy, which incorporates many insights including the freedom to choose one's attitude. We have reviewed Frankl's vast array of books, articles, speeches, and related works and have distilled his teachings into what we believe are the seven most important core principles to help you on your quest for meaning. The "freedom to choose your attitude" is just one of the seven principles that we share in this book. We have also provided a conceptual foundation as well as practical guidance for examining your own questions about meaning.

Our specific goal through this book is to bring meaning to work and the workplace. Because we define *work* very broadly, the message applies to a wide audience: to paid workers as well as to volunteers; to people employed in all sectors and industries; to individuals beginning a job search or a new career; to those in transition; and to retirees. Because the book demonstrates Frankl's principles at work in a general context, these core principles can be applied to life outside the workplace. Examples, stories, exercises, questions, challenges, and other practical tools help guide you in applying Frankl's ideas to finding your own path to meaning at work and in your personal life.

Alex's Perspective on Viktor Frankl

Frankl's influence on my work and personal life goes back almost fifty years. I spent many of these years studying his groundbreaking work in existential analysis, Logotherapy, and the search for meaning, and I have applied his principles in multiple work environments and situations. As a mental health professional, I have relied on the power of Frankl's ideas for years. My reliance has evolved and expanded over time as I have tested elements of his philosophy and approach in a wide variety of organizational settings. Working with individuals experiencing existential dilemmas at work and/or in their personal lives, I naturally have reflected on my own life journey and have frequently relied on and benefited from Frankl's wisdom.

Viktor Frankl practiced what he preached, living and

Dr. Alex Pattakos with Dr. Viktor
Frankl in his study, Vienna, Austria,
August 1996

working with meaning throughout his life. This is not always easy to do, as I know from personal experience. There is a saying in the academic world that we don't know what we don't know until we try to teach it. The same thing can be said about writing a book. And yet in many respects, *writing* a book is the easy part. The really hard part, I must confess, comes when we try to *do* what we write about. I can only try to follow Frankl's lead. It was in a meeting with Frankl at his home in Vienna, Austria, in 1996 when I first proposed the idea of writing a book that would apply his core principles and approach explicitly to work and the workplace. He was more than encouraging—in his typical passionate style, he leaned across his desk, grabbed my arm, and said, "Alex, yours is the book that needs to be written." His words burned into the core of my being, and I was determined from that moment to make this book idea a reality.

I realize now more than ever the good fortune and benefit I have had of metaphorically standing on the shoulders of Viktor Frankl, one of the greatest thinkers of modern times. Through his own story of finding a reason to live despite the horrendous circumstances of Nazi concentration camps, Frankl left a legacy that can help everyone, no matter what their situation, find deeper, richer meaning in their lives. It is my intention and hope that *Prisoners of Our Thoughts* builds upon Frankl's legacy of meaning in life and work, supporting his transformational legacy so it is never forgotten.

Welcome to the Third Edition

Today's fast-changing, increasingly complex, and uncertain world has amplified the interest in the search for meaning in life, work, and society. It is time to extend the life-affirming and inspirational messages from the first and second editions in this third edition. A key change in this edition is the addition of my partner, spouse, and muse, Elaine Dundon, as coauthor. Given her unique background in business, innovation, meaning, philosophy, and metaphysics, Elaine brings an interesting dynamic to this third edition.

Elaine's Perspective on Viktor Frankl

Frankl's influence on my work and personal life can be traced back to my adolescent years when I first read *Man's Search for Meaning*. Since then, I have revisited this seminal book for insights on how to deal with and find meaning in the challenging circumstances I've faced in my personal and work situations. Often I realized that I was a prisoner, not in the literal sense of being behind steel bars and barbed wire, but in the figurative sense of entrapping myself with limiting beliefs—not just about my own circumstances and abilities but also about how I held others as prisoners of my thoughts on how they might continue to behave. Fortuitously, I met

Alex Pattakos and subsequently learned of his interest in the areas of Logotherapy, existential analysis, and the search for meaning in life and work. Together, our odyssey has taken us around the world, where we have had the great fortune to meet so many people interested in sharing their views and insights on meaning and, specifically, on how Frankl's wisdom has helped them overcome challenging situations. It has been an honor and a privilege to advance Frankl's work and, of course, to share the journey with my husband, partner, and sage, Alex.

In this revised and expanded third edition we offer original and updated stories, fresh applications and exercises, and four new chapters ("Meaning at the Core: Life," "Meaning at the Core: Work," "Meaning at the Core: Society," and "Viktor Frankl's Legacy Continues"). We encourage you to *live this book* by reviewing the concepts and examples, practicing the exercises, and adopting the principles in your daily work and life. Only in this way will the book be more than just another book in your library. Only in this way will Frankl's voluminous body of work have the impact it deserves. Only in this way will this book help you truly find deeper meaning in your life and work.

Alex Pattakos, PhD
Elaine Dundon, MBA

Life Doesn't Just Happen to Us

Ultimately, man should not ask what the meaning of his
life is, but rather must recognize that it is he who is asked.
In a word, each man is questioned by life; and he can
only answer to life by answering for his own life; to life
he can only respond by being responsible.[1] (V. Frankl)

It seems that I (Alex) have known Viktor Frankl most of my life. It was in the late 1960s when I first became acquainted with his work and read his classic book *Man's Search for Meaning*. While on active duty with the U.S. Army, I received formal training at Brooke Army Hospital, now called Brooke Army Medical Center, at Fort Sam Houston in San Antonio, Texas, as a social work/psychology specialist. In addition to the opportunity to work side by side with some of the best mental health professionals in the field, this unique learning experience fueled my passion for studying various schools of thought and practice in psychiatry and psychology. Frankl's work in particular had great resonance for me at that time, and it eventually became an integral part of both my personal and professional life.

Over the years, I have had many opportunities to apply

Frankl's teachings in my own life and work. In effect, I have field-tested the validity and reliability of his key principles and techniques, often in comparison with competing schools of thought and in situations that tested the limits of my personal resilience. It didn't take me long to realize the efficacy of his philosophy and approach, and I became a de facto practitioner of Logotherapy long before the idea for this book surfaced in my mind. Many decisive times in my life, including situations that involved work, could easily be described as turbulent and challenging. Such formidable, life-defining moments, although they often lasted much longer than a moment, required a great deal of soul-searching for answers. I remember how truly out of balance—and yes, even lost—I felt at those critical times. I had learned many years ago from Thomas Moore, psychotherapist and author of the best-selling book *Care of the Soul*, that our most soulful times are when we are out of balance rather than when we are in balance. It was especially during these meaning-centered moments, when I was out of balance, that I found myself putting Frankl's philosophy and approach into practice.

I was particularly out of balance in my early twenties, after graduating from college. I was contemplating going to law school after my military service. My father, an engineer, envisioned that someday I would work for him as an attorney specializing in contract law. With his help and at his urging, I took a job with a large engineering and construction firm in New Jersey. However, I did not see myself as a corporate lawyer. Fueled by my active duty with the U.S. Army during the Vietnam era, I was interested in law only as it could be used as an instrument for social policy and social change. This perspective did not bode well for my relationship with my father or my employer.

Although I felt trapped, Frankl's work reminded me that it was my own responsibility how I chose to react to the situation. I knew I had to maintain a positive, resilient attitude and that this experience—a kind of existential dilemma—was actually giving me an opportunity to clarify and confirm my values around the kind of work I wanted to do and *not* do. This meant leaving my relatively secure place of employment and, harder still, standing up to and engaging in many heated arguments with my father so that I could declare the path that *I* wanted to pursue. From this personal and stressful experience, however, I learned that it was worth the risk and effort! How I faced this difficult situation increased my personal resilience for handling other challenges I have encountered throughout my life.

> One may say that instincts are transmitted through the genes,
> and values are transmitted through traditions, but that meanings,
> being unique, are a matter of personal discovery.[2] (V. Frankl)

I (Elaine) too have faced many situations when I felt out of balance or, in some cases, that I was in balance but the rest of the world was not. One day, years ago, at the age of twelve, when I was babysitting for the woman across the street from our home, she turned to me and said, "That's quite an ordeal your mother is facing." The look on my face must have registered confusion, for she responded, "Oh no. You don't know." She was correct, I did *not* know. I did not know that my mother had been diagnosed with breast cancer and the prognosis was not good. Survival was rare back then without the medical treatments and psychological support that we are blessed with today. My parents had decided not to tell any of their children in an effort, I suppose, to protect us from the bad news. In hindsight, I realized that they also may have not known how to react and needed time to deal with their own fears. However, their decision not to discuss the illness simply served to amplify my fear and sense of loneliness, for there was no one to talk to about the situation.

Somehow, we all got through the storm. My mother survived another fourteen years due to her positive attitude, knowing that she needed to stay alive to guide her four children. She practiced Frankl's principles, most notably those of de-reflection (shifting her focus away from her illness onto things that mattered more—i.e., her children) and of self-detachment (looking at herself from a distance with a sense of perspective, including maintaining her sense of humor). I remember her reading Frankl's *Man's Search for Meaning* while sick in bed. I recall saying to her one day, with tears in my eyes, "I don't want you to die." She held my hand and said, jokingly, "But imagine if no one ever died. Imagine if five-hundred-year-olds, or even thousand-year-olds, were walking around the earth. It would be a very strange world!" In her own kind way, my mother was teaching me about the journey of life. Her courage, love, and wisdom did indeed guide me to put life's challenges in perspective and to find the meaning in any situation, however tragic.

> *I am convinced that, in the final analysis, there is no situation that does not contain within it the seed of a meaning.*[3]
> (V. Frankl)

Frankl's thinking has profoundly influenced both of our lives, including our work situations, over the years. This book is a product of our research on Frankl's teachings, including his personal encouragement, as well as our combined experiences applying these teachings in everyday life and work—for ourselves and with others.

In chapter 2 we explore Viktor Frankl's life path. A psychiatrist who suffered through imprisonment in Nazi concentration camps during World War II, Frankl found meaning in spite of—and because of—the suffering all around him. His life's work resulted in the therapeutic approach called Logotherapy, which paved the way for us to know meaning as a foundation of our existence. Frankl was quick to say, however, that traumatic suffering is *not* a prerequisite for finding meaning in our lives. By this he meant that whenever we suffer—no matter what the severity of our suffering is—we have the ability to find meaning in the situation. We also have the ability to find meaning in the good times. Choosing to find meaning, under any circumstance, is the path to a meaningful life. As a mentor and author, and as the creator of Logotherapy, Frankl had a profound impact on many people during his lifetime. His teachings continue to guide and influence people around the world today.

Although Frankl produced a voluminous body of work, he did not distill his teachings down to a list of seven core principles. We have developed the seven principles that best describe his teachings. Throughout this book, we explore each principle one by one. They include:

PRINCIPLE 1. *Exercise the Freedom to Choose Your Attitude* (chapter 3)

We are all free to choose our attitude toward everything that happens to us. This concept is best described by Frankl's famous quotation in his book *Man's Search for Meaning*: "Everything can be taken from a man but . . . the last of the human freedoms—to choose one's attitude in any given set of circumstances, to choose one's way."[4]

PRINCIPLE 2. *Realize Your Will to Meaning* (chapter 4)

Logotherapy, according to Frankl, "considers man as a being whose main concern consists of fulfilling a meaning and in actualizing values, rather than in the mere gratification and satisfaction of drives and instincts."[5] Rather than simply completing tasks to receive rewards such as money, influence, status, or prestige, we can realize our will to deeper meaning by making a conscious, authentic commitment to meaningful values and goals.

PRINCIPLE 3. *Detect the Meaning of Life's Moments* (chapter 5)

Meaning reveals itself to us in everyday life and work, in *all* of life's moments. The fundamental presumption is that only as individuals can we answer for our own lives, detecting in them each moment's meaning and weaving our own unique tapestry of existence.

PRINCIPLE 4. *Don't Work Against Yourself* (chapter 6)

Sometimes our most fervent desires and intentions are thwarted by our obsession with outcomes.

Frankl calls this form of self-sabotage *hyperintention*. In some instances, we actually get results exactly opposite to what we intended, which is called *paradoxical intention*. We can learn to see how we are working against ourselves and focus instead on creating the conditions we want in our lives and work.

PRINCIPLE 5. *Look at Yourself from a Distance* (chapter 7)

Frankl observed: "Only man owns the capacity to detach himself from himself. To look at himself out of some perspective or distance."[6] This notion of *self-detachment* can help us lighten up and not sweat the small stuff. This capacity includes the uniquely human trait known as a sense of humor. Frankl noted that "no animal is capable of laughing, least of all laughing *at itself* or *about itself*."[7] We can learn to look at ourselves from a distance to gain insight and perspective, including laughing at ourselves!

PRINCIPLE 6. *Shift Your Focus of Attention* (chapter 8)

When Viktor Frankl was a prisoner in the Nazi concentration camps, in order to cope with stress, suffering, and conflict, he learned to shift his attention away from the painful situation to other, more appealing circumstances. We can learn to shift our focus accordingly when we are coping with difficult situations.

PRINCIPLE 7. *Extend Beyond Yourself* (chapter 9)

Frankl wrote: "Love is the ultimate and the highest goal to which man can aspire. . . . The salvation of man is through love and in love."[8] Extending beyond ourselves, connecting with and being of service to others, no matter what the situation or scale, is where our deepest meaning can be realized. Self-transcendence, by relating and being directed to something greater than ourselves, provides a pathway to ultimate meaning.

These seven core principles support Frankl's key message that we always have the ability to respond to anything that comes our way in life by exercising our capacity to find meaning. Life doesn't just happen *to* us—we are responsible for our own lives, and it is up to us, like Frankl was able to do even in the Nazi death camps, to actively find meaning in our lives. We cannot be victims, we cannot be passive participants in life and, most of all, we cannot be *prisoners of our thoughts!*

In chapter 10 ("Meaning at the Core: Life"), chapter 11 ("Meaning at the Core: Work"), and chapter 12 ("Meaning at the Core: Society"), we share how Frankl's teachings, along with insights from our own research, writing, and experiences, can help us focus upon and find deeper meaning in life, work, and society. Another key message in this book from Frankl's teachings and our related work is that meaning must be at the *foundation* or *core* of one's life, which includes one's broadly defined work life. Without an understanding of meaning in our lives and work, we are simply like a boat being tossed around at sea without any true connection to others and without a clear direction or purpose to guide us through life's odyssey.

There is a crisis of meaning in the world today. Many people have told us that they feel something is missing. They feel overwhelmed, lonely, and unfulfilled. Generally, they feel disconnected and not fully engaged with their lives or work. Depression is on the rise, and many people simply can't cope with the pace of change brought on by technological, cultural, and social transformations. The relentless pursuit of pleasure and other short-term escapes have only led to even more emptiness. We are told to pursue "happiness," yet happiness is an illusion for many, as it does not take into consideration the natural flow or rhythms of life—the ups and the downs, the joys and the sorrows, the good times and the not-so-good times.

To pursue "happiness" leaves us even more depressed when the state of our lives doesn't measure up to our expectations or falls short of the glorified lives we so often see on Facebook and other social media. The pursuit of power and influence is another illusion. Power is about being strong and dominant, having or trying to have control over others or other things. The pursuit of wealth can be viewed as another form of the pursuit of power. Ultimately, the pursuit of power only leads to frustration because one can never truly control other people or events. A wise person knows that one's only real power lies *within* and *over* oneself.

In chapters 10, 11, and 12, we highlight our work in a new discipline we call MEANINGology®—that is, the study and practice of meaning in life, work, and society. While many people define meaning as "significance" or "something that matters," we delve deeper, in a Logotherapeutic or existential sense, to consider the metaphysical aspects of the entire study of meaning. We define *meaning* as "resonance with our true nature or core essence." When something feels significant or we know that it matters, it is because it resonates with who we truly are. *Core essence* is what defines us and is at the heart of what makes us unique as human beings. This deeper definition of meaning can apply to our personal and work lives, to organizations, and to societies as a whole. It is also beneficial to look at the converse—identifying what is *meaningless* to us or what does *not* resonate with our true nature or core essence. This exercise, among other things, helps us to gain a deeper understanding of the sources of meaning throughout our lives and work.

Another aspect of our MEANINGology work highlighted in chapters 10, 11, and 12 centers on our "formula" for discovering meaning in life and work. While the seven core principles help to focus the learning and discussion of Viktor Frankl's teachings in Logotherapy and Existential Analysis, we felt that there was need for more clarification and guidance on how to put into action the human quest for meaning both individually and collectively. Through our research and experience, we have discovered three elements for finding deeper meaning that can be viewed as an integration, simplification, and extension of the seven Logotherapeutic principles described in the earlier chapters. These three elements are:

- Connect meaningfully with others (O).
- Engage with deeper purpose (P).
- Embrace life with attitude (A).

These elements spell "OPA!"—an easy-to-remember, simple acronym. This mantra for living and working can provide further insights on one's path to meaning. We provide more details about the OPA formula and its practical application in chapters 10, 11, and 12.

Finally, in chapter 13 ("Viktor Frankl's Legacy Continues"), we highlight how Dr. Frankl's legacy continues to expand around the world as the seeds of his System of Logotherapy and Existential Analysis find new soil in which to be planted, cultivated, and harvested. The information contained in this last chapter serves to illustrate that Frankl's memory is eternal, that his wisdom is ageless, and that his life's work continues to influence humanity in significant (i.e., meaningful) ways. But for now, let's take an initial look at Viktor Frankl's life, explore more fully the foundations of his meaning-centered approach, and learn how all of us can apply his groundbreaking philosophy in our own lives.

Meaning Reflections

At the end of each chapter, we have added a section in this third edition called Meaning Reflections, which includes a Meaning Moment Exercise, Meaning Questions, and a Meaning Affirmation—all designed to help you incorporate the key lessons of each chapter into your own life and work.

Meaning Moment Exercise Write down the details of a situation, either in your personal or work life, involving another person whom you have viewed as being particularly negative. Now write down the details of the situation from the other person's point of view. How do these two descriptions differ? Do you view yourself as a victim of circumstances that are outside of your control, or are you in some way responsible for part or all of what happened? What can you learn from this negative situation? What could you have done differently, and what would you do differently if a similar situation were to occur again?

Meaning Questions

- Are you a prisoner of your thoughts?
- Do you hold *other* people (coworkers, family members, friends) prisoners of your thoughts?
- How can you find more meaning in your life and work?

Meaning Affirmation

I will take an active role in and take responsibility for my life as well as exercise my capacity to find meaning, because I know that life doesn't just happen to me.

Viktor Frankl

I do not forget any good deed done to me,
and I carry no grudge for a bad one.[1] (V. Frankl)

Viktor E. Frankl was born in Vienna, Austria, on March 26, 1905. It was the day Beethoven died, and in Frankl's autobiography he is quick to note this coincidence and reveal his sense of humor by sharing a comment made by one of his schoolmates: "One mishap comes seldom alone."[2] Frankl's father, who had been forced to drop out of medical school for financial reasons, was a public servant who instilled in the young Viktor a firm sense of social justice. For thirty-five years Viktor's father worked for the department of child protection and youth welfare. Viktor's mother, with whom he was very close, helped him develop his emotional side—the feelings and human connectedness that would inform his work as deeply as did his rationality.

Frankl was the second of three children, and at an early age he was afflicted with perfectionism. "I do not even speak to myself for days," he said, referring to his anger at himself for not always being perfect. His astonishing and precocious interests in learning about human motivations led him to write to the well-known Viennese psychiatrist and "father of psychoanalysis" Sigmund Freud, with whom he had a correspondence throughout his high school years. Unfortunately this correspondence was lost years later to the Gestapo, the secret-police organization in Nazi Germany and German-occupied Europe.

Young Frankl's own search for meaning was already under way. He had become convinced that the human spirit is what makes us unique and that reducing life and human nature to "nothing but," along the lines of many existentialist philosophers and psychiatrists of his time, denied or discounted any such spirit. At sixteen, he gave his first public lecture, "On the Meaning of Life." Two years later, he wrote "On the Psychology of Philosophical Thought," for his high school graduation essay. It was almost as though on some level Frankl was preparing for the tragedy that lay ahead and the future role he would play in giving hope to all of humankind after the hopelessness and despair of the Holocaust.

In 1924, at Freud's request, Frankl published his first article in the *International Journal of Psychoanalysis*. He was nineteen years old and had already developed two of his fundamental ideas: First, we ourselves are responsible for our own existence, and we must answer the question that life asks us about the meaning of our own lives. Second, although ultimate meaning is beyond our comprehension and must remain so, we must have faith in meaning as we pursue it. Also in 1924, Frankl started his medical studies, and his growing professional recognition included a developing relationship with renowned psychiatrist Alfred Adler. It was Adler who invited him to publish another article, this time in the *International Journal of Individual Psychology*. Frankl still was only twenty years old.

Logotherapy

A year later, during public lectures in Germany, Frankl used the word *Logotherapy* for the first time. He chose this name for his unique approach to a humanistic form of psychotherapy, which came to be known as the "Third Viennese School of Psychotherapy" (the predecessors being the Freudian and Adlerian Schools). This system of psychotherapy paved the way for us to know meaning as the foundation of our existence. Frankl chose this name with direct reference to the Greek word *logos* (λóγος) for several reasons. One was the fact that the most frequent, though rough, English translation of *logos* as "the meaning" best fit his paradigm of "therapy through meaning." We should mention that Frankl was not referring to our modern interpretation and use of the word or term *logos*, which many know as a graphic symbol of a trademark, product, or company name designed for easy recognition. Although this contemporary definition can be associated with the original Greek word by linking the graphic symbol to the deeper meaning of a product or company, Frankl certainly was not speaking about graphically designed logos and our modern-day marketing practices.

Upon closer examination, the various translations of the word *logos* reveal that it has deep spiritual roots.[3] One of the first references to logos as "spirit" came from the ancient Greek philosopher Heraclitus around 500 BC. The logos of

Heraclitus has been interpreted in various ways: as "the logical," as "meaning," and as "reason." To Heraclitus, the logos was responsible for the harmonic order of the universe, a cosmic law that declared, "One Is All and Everything Is One." He believed that there was an order to the universe and a reason for things being the way they are. We can find deeper understanding, and thus meaning in our lives and work, if we start by doing what Heraclitus suggested: believing that all things are connected.

The concept of logos can also be found in many of the great literary works of Western philosophy and religion. The doctrine of the logos was the linchpin of the religious thinking by the Jewish philosopher Philo of Alexandria, who clearly established it as belonging to the spiritual realm. Indeed, for Philo the logos was divine—it was the source of energy from which the human soul became manifest. To Philo, the origins of logos as "spirit" and "life energy" were clearly established and well documented in the writings of the early Greek philosophers and the theologians of his era.[4]

It is no coincidence that the concept and process of dialogue, a core methodological component of Frankl's Logotherapy, likewise is grounded in the logos. The word *dialogue* comes from two Greek words: *dia* (δια), meaning "passing through," and *logos*, translated as "meaning" or "spirit." The process of dialogue takes on a new and deeper meaning when it is perceived as accessing a pool of common spirit (logos) through a genuine connection between people. This suggests more than collective thinking or simply arriving at a common understanding or shared meaning of something. Authentic dialogue enables individuals to acknowledge honestly that each is part of a greater whole, that they naturally resonate with others within this whole, and that the whole is indeed greater than the sum of its various parts. As participants in such a holistic process, together they can produce greater results than they would just as individuals without this meaningful connection.

As we can see, Logotherapy was an appropriate name for Frankl's unique and very humanistic approach to inspiring us to search for and find deeper meaning in our lives and work. It should be noted that he was not an advocate for the practices of traditional psychotherapy at that time, for he felt that many practitioners tended to focus only on a certain aspect of a person's life without regard for his or her whole life. He felt this "reductionist" approach was limited and in some ways dehumanizing. Frankl's work acknowledged human weakness, but it went further—to search for and acknowledge the underlying meaning behind these weaknesses. This approach highlighted the potential benefit to be had when we learn from and even transform our weaknesses. Frankl believed that every event, whether seen as positive or negative, could teach us something about ourselves and our world. "I am convinced," he wrote in his autobiography, "that, in the final analysis, there is no situation that does not contain within it the seed of a meaning."[5]

Frankl encountered many challenges as he attempted to gain support for his innovative meaning-centered therapeutic approach. By the time he received his medical degree in 1930, he had been banished from the Adler circle because he supported an alternative point of view about the fundamental nature of human motivations. His unique existential philosophy also forced him to leave the Freudian circle. As it turned out, the experience of having to leave both well-established camps only helped to pave the way for Frankl to develop his own school of thought and psychotherapeutic approach.

At an early age, Frankl had already gained an international reputation for his work in youth counseling, and from 1930 to 1938 he was on the staff of the psychiatric University Clinic in Vienna. By 1938 he had an established private practice in neurology and psychiatry. However, World War II started, and the Germans invaded Austria. During the early part of the war, Frankl and his family were afforded a measure of protection because of his position as chief of the neurological department at Rothschild Hospital, the only Jewish hospital in Vienna. During this time, he risked his life and saved the lives of many others. On some occasions he used false diagnoses to sabotage the Nazi's efforts to euthanize mentally ill patients. It was during this period that he started writing his first book, *The Doctor and the Soul*.

In September 1942, Frankl and his family were arrested and deported to the Theresienstadt concentration camp near Prague. This was the beginning of three dark years of imprisonment during which Frankl lost his wife, Tilly, his parents, and his brother to the horrors of the Nazi prison camps. He was incarcerated at Auschwitz-Birkenau, Dachau, and finally at Türkheim, where he nearly died from typhoid fever. The Nazis had confiscated the manuscript of his first book, *The Doctor and the Soul*, but Frankl was able to reconstruct it on bits of paper stolen from the camp office. In his autobiography he recollected: "I am convinced that I owe my survival, among other things, to my resolve to reconstruct that lost manuscript."[6]

After his release at the end of the war, Frankl wrote about his experiences in the concentration camps in his book *Man's Search for Meaning*. He wrote graphically and unflinchingly about the treatment, torture, and murder of the prisoners. He also described the beauty of the human spirit, however—how it could transcend the horror and find meaning under the most unimaginable circumstances. Frankl's experiences and observations reinforced the principles of meaning he had developed in his youth. In the death camps of Nazi Germany, he saw men who walked through the huts comforting others, giving away their last piece of bread. "They may have been few in number," he wrote, "but they offer sufficient proof that everything can be taken from a man but one thing: the last of human freedoms—to choose one's attitude in any given set of circumstances, to choose one's own way."[7]

This statement is perhaps one of the most often quoted passages from Frankl's work. U.S. Senator John McCain, for example, attributed his own survival as a prisoner of war in Vietnam for five and a half years in large part to the learning he acquired from Frankl's experience and teachings. In fact, McCain began the preface to his 1999 memoir, *Faith of My Fathers*, with the same Frankl quotation. In Frankl's words: "You do not have to suffer to learn. But, if you don't learn from suffering, over which you have no control, then your life becomes truly meaningless. . . . The way in which a man accepts his fate—those things beyond his control—can add a deeper meaning to his life. He controls how he responds."[8]

At the end of the war, as a survivor and as a psychiatrist, Frankl knew that his theories of Logotherapy had greater authenticity and ever-deeper meaning. He wrote about the ongoing nightmares resulting from his experiences, but he knew those experiences laid the groundwork for his belief in self-transcendence and the will to meaning:

> I can see beyond the misery of the situation to the potential for discovering a meaning behind it, and thus to turn an apparently meaningless suffering into a genuine human achievement. I am convinced that, in the final analysis, there is no situation that does not contain within it the seed of a meaning.[9] (V. Frankl)

Frankl returned to Vienna after the war and became director of the Vienna Neurological Policlinic, a position he held for twenty-five years. He started a long and distinguished academic career that took him to the University of Vienna, Harvard University, and many other universities throughout the world. He received twenty-nine honorary doctorates during his life and wrote thirty-two books, which have been translated into twenty-seven languages. His Man's Search for Meaning is considered by the Library of Congress to be one of the ten most influential books in America. Because he went through the hell of despair over the apparent meaninglessness of life—and struggled with the pessimism associated with such a reductionist and ultimately nihilistic view of life—Frankl was able to fully develop and refine his therapeutic system of Logotherapy. At a conference in San Diego in 1980, Frankl said that he had wrestled with this view that undercut faith in life's meaning, like Jacob did with the angel, until he could "say yes to life in spite of everything." Interestingly, an earlier version of Man's Search for Meaning had this very quotation as its title.

In 1992 the Viktor Frankl Institute was established in Vienna. Today the institute continues to serve as the center of a worldwide network of research and training institutes and societies dedicated to advancing his philosophy and therapeutic system of Logotherapy and Existential Analysis. Viktor Frankl died peacefully on September 2, 1997, at the age of ninety-two. He remained creative, productive, and passionate to the end of his life.

Meaning Reflections

Meaning Moment Exercise Recall a situation in your personal life or work in which you felt trapped, confined, or imprisoned. Perhaps you just didn't have the freedom or authority to deal with the situation in the way that ideally you would have liked. What, if anything, did you do about it? As you think about the situation now, what did you learn from it? In hindsight, what could you have done differently?

Meaning Questions

- Consider the hardships you have experienced in your personal and work life. How might Frankl's experience in the concentration camps help you deal with such hardships (to settle the memories of the past and to deal with challenges in the present and the future)?
- What is your vision of the kind of work that you really want to do and the kind of life that you really would like to live?

Meaning Affirmation

I will appreciate the freedom I do have in my life.

Viktor Frankl

PRINCIPLE 1. Exercise the Freedom to Choose Your Attitude

Everything can be taken from a man but . . . the last of the human freedoms—to choose one's attitude in any given set of circumstances, to choose one's way.[1] (V. Frankl)

Human beings are, by nature, creatures of habit. Searching for a life that is both predictable and within our comfort zone, we rely on routine and, for the most part, learned thinking patterns. We create pathways in our minds in much the same way that a path is beaten through a grass field from repeated use. Because these patterns are automatic, we may believe these habitual ways of thinking and behaving to be beyond our control. Thus we rationalize our responses to life and fall prey to forces that limit our potential as human beings. By viewing ourselves as relatively powerless and driven by instinct, the possibility that we can create, or at least *co-create*, our own reality becomes difficult to grasp. Instead, we often lock ourselves inside our own mental prisons. We lose sight of our own natural potential and that of others. In essence, we become prisoners of our thoughts.

Yet we can reshape our patterns of thinking. Through our own search for meaning, we can unfreeze ourselves from our limited perspective, find the key, and unlock the door of our metaphorical prison cell. We can change our perspective once we realize that we do, indeed, have the freedom to choose our attitude toward whatever is happening in our lives.

> *Each of us has his own inner concentration camp . . . we must deal with, with forgiveness and patience—as full human beings; as we are and what we will become.*[2] (V. Frankl)

The responsibility for choosing our attitude lies solely with each of us. It cannot be transferred to someone else. This ultimate responsibility applies both to our personal and our work lives. We have made this claim over the years to various business and government clients, especially in cases where workers, including executives and managers, seem intent on complaining about their working conditions rather than doing anything to change the situation. We all know people who habitually define their work or job in a negative way.

Take, for example, Bob, who would appear to many to be a fairly successful bank executive. However, his work journey has taken him through some dramatic twists and turns, causing him much stress. Bob rarely, if ever, seems positive or optimistic about his job and, by extension, his life. He complains incessantly about his responsibilities, his colleagues, his customers, his community, and just about every other aspect of his working life. Bob's colleagues and family hear nothing but stories of misery, negativity, and despair. Unfortunately, Bob seems unable and unwilling to see that he is creating his own reality, that his constant complaining is hampering his work success and negatively affecting his family and his personal life. One by one, Bob's friends have drifted away from him, not wanting to surround themselves with such negativity. His family perseveres, enduring through a sense of obligation but certainly not through a sense of joy.

Complaining about a miserable job around the watercooler or starting a "bitch and moan club" at the office might offer moments of camaraderie, but it doesn't nurture meaning—for oneself or for others. The idea that work is neither fun nor fulfilling takes a huge toll on our ability to bring meaning to our work. When we habitually complain, we make meaninglessness a habit. Before long, we are so deeply invested in complaining that any opportunity to see the work experience as a rich part of our lives vanishes. Instead of taking the time to find meaning, we take the time to find and focus on meaninglessness. Such complaints trivialize our experiences—both at work and in our personal lives. When we complain, we disconnect. When we complain, we hold whatever or whoever we're complaining about as a shield. We therefore perpetuate victimization and helplessness.

What is a serial complainer to do? The first task is to become aware of when and why we are complaining. The second task is to stop complaining! This doesn't mean we won't complain once in a while; it means that we become aware of when we are complaining and that we are choosing to complain, choosing to be negative. This does not mean that we deny our burdens, our grief, and our worries and sign on to a Pollyannaish, blindly optimistic perspective of the world. Viktor Frankl certainly had the opportunity to complain. He could have chosen to be negative. However, he excavated the darkest despair and discovered meaning in his circumstances. He didn't have to create the meaning—it was there waiting to be found. He knew well the meaning of unavoidable suffering through his experience in the Nazi concentration camps. He knew the darkest human behavior and, at the same time, the brightest light of human possibility. Frankl carried the awareness of both potentialities, which deepened his humanity and created in him a deep and abiding faith. He saw people rise out of the most depraved circumstances and offer all they had to others. Viktor Frankl saw the manifestation of spirit on a daily basis.

When we recognize that we always have the ultimate freedom to choose our attitude, we are free to choose whether it will be negative or positive. By releasing our negative attitude, we release energy that can then be used to connect more meaningfully with others. When we authentically connect more deeply with others, we create a new community of support and possibility. When we make this kind of authentic connection, we can't avoid meaning. It's waiting for us around every watercooler, in every elevator, cubbyhole, taxicab, conference room, and corporate boardroom. When we open ourselves to meaning, when we stop to appreciate ourselves and others in meaningful ways, we immediately enhance the quality of our own lives as well as the lives of those around us.

A Lesson in True Freedom

There is an inspiring story about Nelson Mandela, the first black president of South Africa and winner of the Nobel Peace Prize, which meaningfully illuminates the relationship between personal freedom and imprisonment. At a young age, Mandela fought to change South Africa's economically and politically oppressive apartheid system and to foster racial equality. In 1962 he was arrested, convicted of conspiracy to overthrow the state, and sentenced to life imprisonment. As a result of mounting pressure from the people of South Africa and international agencies, Mandela was released from prison in 1990 after serving twenty-seven years.

The day Mandela was released from prison, Bill Clinton, then governor of Arkansas, was watching the news. Clinton called to his wife and daughter: "You must see this; it is historic." As Mandela stepped out from the prison walls to be greeted by the international press, Clinton saw a flush of anger on Mandela's face as he looked at the people watching. But then the anger disappeared. Later, when Clinton was president of the United States and Mandela was president of South Africa, the two leaders met, and Clinton relayed this observation. Clinton candidly asked Mandela to explain what seemed to have occurred on that day. Mandela replied: "Yes, you are right. When I was in prison, the son of a guard started a Bible study and I attended; . . . and that day when I stepped out of prison and looked at the people observing, a flush of anger hit me with the thought that they had robbed me of twenty-seven years. Then the Spirit of Jesus said to me, 'Nelson, while you were in prison you were free; now that you are free, don't become their prisoner.'"[3] Indeed, upon his release Mandela displayed his ability, once again, to be a model for reconciliation, with no spirit of revenge or negativism. He understood that the freedom to choose one's attitude is one of the most basic and important freedoms human beings have.

It's neither proper nor possible to compare the ways in which Viktor Frankl and Nelson Mandela endured unthinkable experiences. But they represent all people who have experienced suffering and triumphed, each in his or her own way. These people were compelled, under uniquely dreadful circumstances, to find meaning within their imprisoned lives. Stripped of most of the freedoms many of us take for granted, as prison inmates these two men were left with what Frankl called the "last of the human freedoms"—the freedom to choose one's attitude in response to life circumstances. This freedom to choose is available to us all, in every aspect of our lives. Yet it can be difficult, when our lives are comparably safe and perceivably free, to do so. We all struggle with situations beyond our control. Bringing these aspects of our lives under control—even if it is only our attitude toward a particular situation—is where our freedom takes shape, no matter what the circumstances.

The Real Superman

The late actor Christopher Reeve had it all. In addition to his early success on Broadway, he was known all over the world for his leading role in *Superman*, the 1978 movie that made him a star. At the age of forty-two, his acting career was bright and his life was filled with unlimited possibilities. He was passionate about life and was intent on experiencing it with gusto. An all-around athlete, Reeve loved sailing and was a skilled equestrian, skier, ice skater, and tennis player. On Memorial Day 1995, however, the world held its breath as Reeve struggled for life. He had been thrown from his horse in an accident that broke his neck, leaving him unable to move or breathe on his own. The man who was Superman had become quadriplegic.

Despite the tragic accident, as he wrote in his best-selling autobiography, appropriately titled *Still Me*: "I think a hero is an ordinary individual who finds strength to persevere and endure in spite of overwhelming obstacles."[4] And so the story of the real Superman continued. In the years after the accident, Reeve not only survived but also thrived—fighting for himself, for his family, and for thousands of people with spinal cord injuries in the United States and around the world. An inspirational force, Reeve displayed his choice to maintain a positive attitude toward his situation on *Larry King Live*, just ten months after the accident: "I am a very lucky guy," he said. "I can testify before Congress. I can raise funds. I can raise awareness."[5] Reeve credited his wife, Dana, and his three children for lifting him out of an initial morass of hopelessness. "You learn the stuff of your life (sports, movies) . . . that's not the essence of your existence," he said. "My relationships were always good. Now they have transcended. That's why I can honestly say I am a lucky man." He went further:

When a catastrophe happens, it's easy to feel so sorry for yourself that you can't see anybody around you. But the way out is through your relationships. The way out of that misery or obsession is to focus more on what your little boy needs or what your teenagers need or what other people around you need. It's very hard to do, and often you have to force yourself. But that is the answer to the dilemma of being frozen—at least it's the answer I found.[6]

Christopher Reeve exercised his freedom to choose his attitude about his life and work, which enabled him to take the bold steps of confronting the unforeseen changes in his path. By doing so, he was able to do more than simply cope with his personal suffering and loss. He unleashed his potential for self-healing and discovered a path to authentic meaning that might have gone unnoticed. As a by-product of his conscious choice, Reeve was able to remind us that life is not to be taken for granted but to be lived fully, with passion, curiosity, and gratitude.[7] He chose to live with a positive attitude until his death in 2004, at the age of fifty-two.

Christopher Reeve was an inspirational role model for others. Most notably, his positive attitude directly influenced his wife, Dana, who took care of him for almost ten years after the accident. Dana experienced another personal tragedy in August 2005: even though she had never smoked in her life, she was diagnosed with lung cancer. Despite enduring personal tragedies, Dana chose to face life with strength and courage. When she was asked how she maintained such a positive outlook, Dana replied that she had had a "good teacher"—her husband. The American actress, singer, activist for disability causes, and wife of the real Superman died on March 6, 2006, at the age of forty-four.

Learning to Cope

As we venture through life, we encounter both joyful and sorrowful times. Although we might wish to experience only the happy times, we know that to live a full life, we must be prepared to experience challenging and often painful situations. Life is about opposites: day and night, sickness and health, good and evil, wealth and poverty, and so on. Opposites are beneficial because they help us define and contrast things; we need to know one in order to know the other. Life is about embracing both the joys and the challenges, not simply going through the motions. It is the wholeness of life that we should be embracing. It is in the wholeness of life that we build our resilience and coping abilities to face all of life's challenges. It is in the wholeness of life that we experience the most meaning.

In Viktor Frankl's case, had he not understood the totality of life, the joys and the challenges, he might not have been able to survive the horrid conditions of the concentration camps. Had he not adopted his overall beliefs about coping before his arrival at Auschwitz, he might not have been able to sustain his optimistic and passionate view about his own chances of survival:

> Unless there was a 100 percent guarantee that I will be killed here on the spot, and I will never survive this concentration camp last part of my life, unless there is any guarantee, I'm responsible for living from now on in a way that I may make use of the slightest chance of survival, ignoring the great danger surrounding me in also all the following camps I had been sent. This, as it were, a coping, not mechanism, but a coping maxim I adopted, I espoused, at that moment.[8] (V. Frankl)

Here Frankl refers to what he called his *coping maxim*, an overarching set of fundamental principles (or rules of conduct) that helped him handle the formidable challenges he faced. By responsibly choosing and authentically committing to his fundamental attitude about the need for survival upfront, Frankl gained confidence that he would be able to cope with and survive yet another day in the camps.

In life and in the workplace, some individuals cope more easily than others with changes in circumstances. In many instances, the most capable, responsible, and resilient individuals have adopted a coping maxim (an overall belief about coping), confidence that they can cope, and skills to guide them through life's challenges and toward more meaning in the present day and for the future. It is important to ask ourselves, What are our coping maxims and what are our beliefs about our ability to cope in challenging circumstances?

True Optimism

Being a true optimist requires more than just positive thinking. Positive affirmations (like the ones included at the end of each chapter in this book, starting with the words, *I will . . .*) are useful, even beneficial, as a starting point when we face the challenges that come our way in life and work. However, like good intentions, positive affirmations are not enough in and of themselves. They must be supported by two other steps: our ability to *visualize* the possibilities for dealing with the situation at hand resulting from our choice of attitude and, importantly, our *passion* for taking the action required to actualize those possibilities. In other words, when we choose our attitude in light of what we call "true optimism," we actually make three choices:

1. We choose a positive attitude about the situation at hand.
2. We choose to visualize what's possible to deal with the situation at hand.
3. We choose an attitude that generates passion for the action that makes the possible become a reality.

All of us have the freedom to make these choices, but it is amazing how frequently we don't. We either choose to abstain from taking full responsibility for what should be our conscious choice, or we choose, albeit unconsciously, to remain frozen in thought patterns that may no longer serve our highest good. In short, we become *prisoners of our thoughts*.

In our life and throughout our work on finding meaning, we have encountered clients, coworkers, friends, and family members who are stuck in old habits of self-imprisonment. They display the power of *negative* thinking about a work or life situation, ensuring that they could never visualize a better tomorrow. Or they are so fearful of the unknown that they have essentially immobilized themselves, effectively avoiding any kind of risk. The ultimate freedom to choose their attitude and their future, no matter how desperate they may be, seems as foreign to them as a life in which they could feel fulfilled and happy. For example, Tom was unhappy with his job and although he discussed leaving his company on many occasions, he could not bring himself to make the decision to move on. He seemed unable to visualize future possibilities and stated that he could not see himself doing anything else.

One day, Tom's organization decided to downsize and he, among many others, was let go after years of faithful service. Although Tom did not agree with the company's decision to release him, and he felt that his value was neither acknowledged nor fully understood, he realized that he was given no choice but to move on. Tom came to terms with the company's decision and forced himself to change his attitude. "Maybe uncertainty brings out the best in us," he professed. Forced to take a leap, Tom shifted to a positive attitude about his newfound freedom and began to visualize the various options he had for work. He is now combining several opportunities that more accurately reflect his deep passion, values, and interests. Ironically, it took the company's decision to let Tom go before he was able to see the need to shift his attitude and to pursue work that was more meaningful and more in line with his true interests.

Much has been written about retirement and the negative effects that retiring can have on people's attitudes and motivations. Use of the word *retire*, which actually means "to withdraw," may be part of the problem. In our opinion, too much focus has been placed on the financial aspect of retirement (Will I have enough money to pay for my expenses until I die?) versus the larger, more existential challenge (How can I best find deeper meaning in the time that remains?). The three steps to true optimism detailed earlier in this chapter can also apply to us as we age. One of our good friends and colleagues, Rebecca, led an adventurous and very eventful life. Always one to focus on the good in life, she chose work that allowed her to express her creative spirit and be a source of insight and inspiration for others. As a creativity consultant, Rebecca advised individuals and organizations on how to move past such mental blocks as "I've always done it that way" and "That can never work" to explore alternative paths. She loved her work—it nourished her soul and brought her great joy as she witnessed her clients' creative-thinking breakthroughs.

Unfortunately, Rebecca experienced a severe hip injury, which confined her to a wheelchair and restricted her ability to move around, to enjoy her active life, and, importantly, to travel to visit her clients. Not letting her injury stop her, Rebecca displayed a strong understanding of the three steps to true optimism:

1. She choose a positive attitude about the physical impairment she was facing.
2. She chose to visualize alternative avenues of creative expression, including beginning to write about her creative-thinking methods in journals to be distributed to her clients.
3. She chose an attitude that generated passion for action instead of feeling stuck or sorry for herself.

More than simply relying on positive thinking alone, Rebecca exercised the freedom to choose her attitude under difficult circumstances. Thus she expanded her life creatively in a new way. She did all this at the age of eighty-nine!

Another person demonstrating the ageless wisdom of

true optimism was Ralph Waldo McBurney, known by friends as Waldo. In October 2006 he was recognized by Experience Works as the oldest worker in America. At the time 104 years old, Waldo was admired as a national symbol for his longevity and work ethic. Waldo, an avid runner, set international records in track and field events and was still competing well after his 101st birthday! One of the most remarkable things about him and his story, however, is that he published his first book in 2004 with the inspirational title *My First 100 Years!* What a true optimist! Although he left us in July 2009, at almost 107 years old, Waldo's life-affirming legacy will live forever. We should all remember Rebecca and Waldo when we hear someone say that they are too old to start something new. It's all about attitude and being a true optimist!

Ten Positive Things Exercise

One of the simplest yet most powerful tools we use to reinforce and apply the "Exercise the Freedom to Choose Your Attitude" principle is our "Ten Positive Things Exercise." To begin, think of a situation in your personal life or at work that is particularly stressful, negative, or challenging for you. Now write ten positive things that resulted from or could result from this situation. Write down any thoughts that come to mind, without filtering them for realism or social acceptance. Try to list as many positives as you can, going beyond ten if possible. Feel free to determine or define what "positive" means to you. After you have completed your list, review it and let the positives become possibilities in your mind. This requires letting go of your current blocked or old ways of thinking, moving beyond disappointment or frustration, and perhaps even abandoning anger. This exercise can open you to a higher level of optimism, no matter how challenging your personal circumstance.

The "Ten Positive Things Exercise" can be applied to many situations. Imagine doing this exercise with this instruction: List ten positive things that would happen if you died today. Most people are not used to discussing, contemplating, and exploring the positives associated with someone's death, let alone their own! Having done this exercise with many groups, we can assure you that once people get over the initial shock and resistance, they relax and actually have a great deal of fun looking for the positives in what is perhaps the most catastrophic situation imaginable. Many people start to see a silver lining or hopeful side in something even as terrible as their own deaths. On one occasion, we had a participant state as a positive: "My wife can finally marry the person she always wanted to marry!"

If we can find something positive to say about our own death, it should be easier to find something positive about our work situation, family life, and so forth. Use this exercise to help you find the positives in such varying and challenging circumstances as losing your job, being in a car accident, and others. Try these:

- List ten positive things that would happen if you lost your job today.

- List ten positive things that would happen if your department at work was eliminated.

- List ten positive things that would happen from a breakdown in the production line at work.

Principle 1. Exercise the Freedom to Choose Your Attitude

- List ten positive things that would happen with an across-the-board 20 percent budget cut at work.

- List ten positive things that would happen if you were in a car accident.

- List ten positive things that would happen if your credit card was lost.

- List ten positive things that would happen if your romantic relationship ended today.

- List ten positive things that would happen if you gained weight.

Each of these situations can be viewed from many different perspectives. No matter how desperate the situation or condition may be, we can always find something positive upon which to focus our attention. When we view the situation in a different light, new ideas, solutions, and opportunities are more likely to come to the surface. Our experience with conducting this exercise in group settings has shown that the positive energy among participants increases dramatically as they learn new things about themselves, each other, and the specific situation they are facing. Everyone learns to release themselves from their self-imposed thought prisons and, as a result, recognizes that ultimately we are all free to choose our attitude, no matter what the circumstance.

Exercise in Action

We have effectively used the "Ten Positive Things Exercise" in many different settings, in a wide variety of life and work situations. This section offers three examples of the exercise in action. The first situation involved a client-training session we were conducting in Alaska with the U.S. Forest Service. At the end of the first day of a two-day session, we overheard comments from one of the more reluctant participants, Paul; he was not interested in the training and didn't feel that it was relevant to him. The "Ten Positive Things Exercise" had been introduced and practiced that afternoon, and Paul obviously was not impressed.

The next morning when we returned to the training venue, we noticed Paul sitting beside two other participants, laughing. When we asked him what had happened, he reported that when he went home the evening after our session, he was shocked to learn that his teenage daughter had received a tongue piercing and was now sporting a new piece of jewelry in her mouth. Angry and upset, Paul argued with his daughter and wife; in short, he had a terrible night with his family. When he returned to the training session, looking tired and depressed, he confessed to his two coworkers what had happened. Immediately, they asked him to list ten positive things that might result from his daughter's action of piercing her tongue. Working together, he and his coworkers identified many potential positives to be gained from Paul's stressful experience (for example, his daughter was alive, she wasn't pregnant, she wasn't in jail, she had shared this event with him, and so on). By looking at these optimistic realities, Paul fostered an entirely new and positive attitude toward his daughter and even our training session! Doing this exercise put this situation in perspective for Paul and helped him to see that things could have been worse for his teenage daughter. He soon changed his attitude about the piercing.

The second example involves a unique twist. I (Alex) had been asked to conduct a workshop on the principles outlined in *Prisoners of Our Thoughts* for inmates at a state penitentiary. The idea of discussing ways to escape one's inner mental prison with actual inmates, some of whom had been sentenced to serve years in prison, was an unusual and challenging opportunity. "Okay, everyone, I would like you to list ten positive things about being in prison," I told the group of about two dozen inmates, who looked at me like I was crazy. In a room designated primarily for education and training purposes, the inmates sat at tables arranged in a circle. Each participant had been given a pad of paper and a small pencil (confiscated at the end of the session for security reasons). They began writing. Some inmates grumbled and others laughed at what they had been asked to do, but all of them participated in the exercise in one way or another.

As expected, some participants were unable to find anything positive in their incarceration, at least not until they heard what their fellow inmates had to say. Some inmates were very serious in the way they framed their responses to this exercise, while others let their imaginations soar with a sense of humor that might have seemed out of place under such circumstances. Here are some examples across the spectrum of what they shared:

- "Society is now protected from me since I'm locked up."
- "I now know what I don't want to do with (the rest of) my life."
- "I can be a role model for others so that they don't do what I did."

- "I'm no longer homeless."
- "I've learned who my real friends are and who aren't."
- "I've been reborn and now value life and freedom like never before."
- "I get to work out a lot."

Of course, these reflections comprise only a snapshot of what the participants shared. The exercise lifted the heavy weight of the energy in the room and tapped into the human spirit. The participants no longer had to think and act only as prison inmates, so each person could experience, even with a sense of humor, the sharing of his authentic thoughts and feelings with the others. The experience enabled them to explore what some might call the silver lining in their current predicament. By being challenged *not* to be prisoners of their thoughts, each participant had the chance to exercise the freedom to choose his attitude despite the circumstance of being incarcerated in an actual prison.

Our third example of using the "Ten Positive Things Exercise" involves a reader of an earlier edition of *Prisoners of Our Thoughts* who faced a very difficult circumstance. Mark had just learned that his wife of twenty-four years had been diagnosed with an aggressive form of breast cancer, found in two spots, one of which was invasive. Mark was devastated. He experienced shock and disbelief, along with a heavy dose of denial, followed by what he described as "god-awful anxiety." For several days after learning about his wife's disease ("the longest days of my life"), Mark couldn't stop crying. In short, he didn't know what to do.

In the midst of his despair, however, Mark remembered the "Ten Positive Things Exercise" and decided along with his wife to give it a shot. We are thankful to them both for sharing the following examples from their longer list of positives. In Mark's words:

1. My wife went by herself for the biopsy results. At first, I was angry as I felt it was my place to accompany her. Then I had the realization that for her, it was an act of bravery to spare me. She called one of my friends at work and asked him to come to my office so that I wouldn't be alone when she phoned me with the bad news. I'm privileged to have a marriage where a spouse can demonstrate that depth of caring for me.

2. Two years ago, I (Mark) went through a challenging double hip replacement. The surgery, rehabilitation, pain tolerance, etc., took about twelve weeks. One achieves a sense of almost total normalcy in about a year. During this time I took the opportunity to lose weight, improve my health, and get as fit as I've ever been in my life. Somehow, in some way, I'm wondering if all of this took place first as preparation for the battle to come. If I ever needed to be physically ready, now is the time.

3. Family, neighbors, and friends have drawn together as a tribe united in a sacred battle to save my wife's life. I've witnessed so many people demonstrate their support and caring that I'm left somewhat speechless. My wife is fiercely loved by many, many people and I, too, am the recipient of their support.

4. It's almost as if my whole life has been a preparation for this test. In some uncanny way I feel like this is exactly where I belong. Make no mistake, I'm terrified. But I'm also resolved to stand my ground with her come what may.

5. I tend to be a skeptic and somewhat pessimistic by nature. Right now, my wife is asking me to help her attach to her anger. She wants to fight and she wants me to get her mad enough to survive. I am now being given the supreme opportunity to relentlessly practice being positive, day in and day out. Minute by minute. If ever I had a moment of swallowing my fear and acting in spite of it, this was it.

6. She and I have confirmed how close we are, but our intimacy is only going to increase in the days ahead. Love is a profoundly mysterious thing.

7. As humans, we tend to see a lifespan as having a narrative arc—from childhood to old age. Any interruption of the unfolding story is seen as tragic. Maybe that's not it at all. Maybe the universe exists because goodness requires it. And maybe what it's all about is that humans were to evolve to discover/create love and meaning—because that's God's nature expressing itself. If that's at least possible, then my wife has accomplished many lifetimes already through her children, her friends, and her relationship with me. That can never be undone; it exists forever.

As Viktor Frankl advised, the way that people accept their fate—those things beyond their control—can add deeper meaning to their life. Such has proven to be the case for Mark and his wife. Through their inescapable suffering, their lives have been enriched with newfound meaning. As Mark and his wife continue to wage their battle with the disease and seek a path to recovery, this meaning will always be with them, providing much-needed support and strength along the way.

Freedom to Choose Our Attitude

One day, I (Alex) had a conversation with a reader of an earlier edition of *Prisoners of Our Thoughts*. A physician, he said, "Alex, I really like your book. I only have one question. I don't really understand the first principle: Exercise the freedom to choose your attitude. Why would I want to do that if I already have an attitude?" Obviously, this particular reader didn't get the message that we are trying to convey! Fortunately, after some discussion, he came to understand the *meaning* behind the principle and has since used it effectively to deal with challenges in his medical practice as well as in his personal life. As Frankl explained:

> As a human phenomenon, however, freedom is all too human. Human freedom is finite freedom. Man is not free from conditions. But he is free to take a stand in regard to them. The conditions do not completely condition him. Within limits it is up to him whether or not he succumbs and surrenders to the conditions. He may as well rise above them and by so doing open up and enter the human dimension. . . . Ultimately, man is not subject to the conditions that confront him; rather, these conditions are subject to his decision. Wittingly or unwittingly, he decides whether he will face up or give in, whether or not he will let himself be determined by the conditions.[9] (V. Frankl)

Although human beings may not be in control of the conditions or situations that confront us, the important thing is that we can choose how we respond, at least through our choice of attitude. According to Frankl, this is not only our right as human beings, it is our full *human beingness* to be free in this manner. All we have to do is resist the temptation of remaining prisoners of our thoughts and choose this freedom, no matter what.

Meaning Reflections

Meaning Moment Exercise Think of a situation that is particularly challenging for you. Now write down ten positive things about this situation. Review and use your list to shift your attitude by identifying new thoughts or perspectives that will open the door to novel solutions to your challenge.

- How do you deal with negativity and complaining from others in your workplace or personal life?
- Are you a complainer? Why do you complain? What is the payoff from your complaining? Are you willing to change your attitude? If so, what steps can you take to change your attitude?
- How do you maintain a positive attitude in your personal life and at work?

Meaning Affirmation

I will choose a positive attitude, visualize possibilities for the future, and take action to make them happen.

PRINCIPLE 2.
Realize Your Will to Meaning

A man who becomes conscious of the responsibility he bears toward a human being who affectionately waits for him, or to an unfinished work, will never be able to throw away his life. He knows the "why" for his existence, and will be able to bear almost any "how."[1] (V. Frankl)

"Oh, I am so happy," Olivia exclaimed. "I have always wanted a Rolex watch. I can hardly wait to show my friends." Many of us can relate to the excitement of getting something new, especially if we had focused our intentions of acquiring it for quite some time. It is the *promise*, the anticipation of pleasure that lures us. But pleasure itself is fleeting and often hard to capture. Although we may have been excited about the prospect of receiving something pleasurable, the feeling of elation quickly dissipates, ultimately leaving us dissatisfied. Many of us get hooked on this cycle—reveling in the anticipation of pleasure, delighting in the buildup and the thrill of the actual event, but inevitably becoming disillusioned when the novelty subsides. It becomes a vicious cycle, a roller coaster, as we seek to experience the euphoric highs of pleasure once more. This situation reminds us of the story of the Greek hero Sisyphus who was ordered by the gods to push a boulder uphill, only to see it slip out of his hands and roll back down the hill, again and again. Similarly, in our quest for happiness and pleasure, life can become an endless and joyless undertaking.

Will to Pleasure

Happiness and pleasure are essential to life, but the challenge with both notions is that they are short-term feelings that come and go depending on our circumstances. We may feel content and happy at certain moments in our lives but these are *feelings* of contentment and happiness, not deep or intrinsic meaning. Happiness and pleasure are essentially illusions, moving targets, dictated by things, events, and other people, external to our real selves. Focusing only on pleasure has its downfalls. If we only seek pleasure, we ignore and even discount the natural rhythm of life—the ups and downs, the joys and sorrows. If we only seek pleasure, we may avoid confrontation or conflict in our relationships, choosing instead to sweep issues under the rug. But, in doing so, we avoid having the conversations that could actually lead to deeper, more authentic relationships and help us grow emotionally and spiritually. If we only seek pleasure, we may miss the opportunity to practice building or strengthening our resilience and our ability to cope—necessary skills for dealing with life's challenges.

When discussing pleasure, many people reference the ancient Greek philosopher Epicurus, who is often associated with hedonism. *Hedonism* is defined as behaving in ways that enable you to get as much pleasure out of life as possible. An *epicurean* is known as a connoisseur of the arts of life, including overindulging in the pleasures of decadent food and drink. In reality, Epicurus's original philosophy centered more on the belief that a pleasant life was one in which we *abstain* from unnecessary desires and actually focus on inner tranquility or calm, being content with simple things. He believed we should choose deep friendships over the fleeting pleasures of food, drink, and sex. He suggested that the way to *real* pleasure was to live modestly and in control of one's desires. A basic tenet of his philosophy was that we can achieve pleasure by avoiding pain. (This aspect of Epicurus's philosophy may have led to the confusion about his teachings. Some people may have understood that in order to avoid the pain [say, the pain of hunger], they should indulge and even overindulge in food. Over time, this misunderstanding—to indulge in food—took center stage in the memory of Epicurus's teachings on pleasure.)

Sigmund Freud, from Vienna, Austria, who was a contemporary and early mentor of Viktor Frankl, also focused on the pursuit of pleasure as a primary motivation of human beings. Writing about the "pleasure principle," Freud suggested, like Epicurus, that the mind naturally or instinctively seeks to maximize pleasure and avoid pain. He believed that humans are programmed to seek instant gratification through the pursuit of pleasure, and only through understanding and maturity can we learn to deter or postpone gratification of this basic human need. As the father of psychoanalysis (a clinical method focused on dialogue between a patient and a psychoanalyst), Freud spent many years examining the *will to pleasure*, espousing it as an integral part of his theory of human motivation.

Unlike most supporters of Freud and his theories, Viktor Frankl followed another path. He developed his own school of thought regarding human motivation and the practice of psychotherapy. Rather than holding a "reductionist" view of human nature that focused on the gratification of drives and instincts, such as those associated with the will to pleasure, Frankl firmly believed that the human potential to realize a *will to meaning*—that is, the authentic commitment to meaningful values and goals—was the primary, intrinsic motivation of human beings. Put differently, Frankl viewed the human condition from a holistic, integrative perspective. He did not agree with Freud that human behavior, like mice in a maze, was simply a function of what he called "secondary rationalization of instinctual drives."[2] As a result of their philosophical differences and divergent perspectives on the aim of psychotherapy, Freud and Frankl parted ways.

Will to Power

Alfred Adler, another Viennese psychiatrist and an early mentor of Viktor Frankl, had developed a school of thought and approach to psychotherapy that focused on the *will to power* as the key driver of human motivation. Known as the founder of individual psychology, Adler believed that we all are born with feelings of inferiority and, as a result, we spend our lives trying to overcome these feelings by striving for superiority. In essence, the will to power viewed humans as being motivated primarily by the need for influence and control over others and their environment. To Frankl, however,

Adler's relentless pursuit of power, much like Freud's pleasure principle (the "will to pleasure"), was a sign that something was missing and was really an attempt to cover up—but not necessarily fill—a void of *meaning*.

Bullying is a common issue in today's society regarding the use and misuse of power. A bully is someone who uses force, threats, manipulation, and coercion in an attempt to intimidate or dominate others. There is an increase in reported cases of bullying in our schools as well as in our workplaces. Bullies use various power tactics, such as spreading malicious gossip, excessive criticism, withholding resources or information, excluding a targeted person from the group, and other devious behaviors intended to undermine the confidence and performance of others. Bullies often take aggressive action against individuals in an effort to control and have power over them.

The root causes of bullying behavior can be traced to a lack of the bully's own self-confidence and other insecurities, their fear of failure, and, in some cases, their attempt to overcompensate for memories of powerlessness when someone else took power away from them, in their earlier years. In a strange way, some people seek conflict—it's part of a lifelong habit or pattern of thinking, feeling, and acting that makes them feel more alive. Without conflict, they feel powerless and miserable, so they continue the cycle of searching for even more conflict. Although they may be stuck in self-defeating behaviors, many bullies lack the self-awareness and insight to see how their power plays are destructive, not only to themselves but to others around them. (The best way to combat bullies is to avoid them, but if you are confronted, it may be beneficial to hold on to your own power—stand up, be assertive, and do not be a victim of their schemes.)

The unending, heartless pursuit of money is also, as Frankl believed, a primitive form of the will to power. In our culture, many have been conditioned to believe that monetary wealth and materialism are symbols of success—the more, the better. Having money and things has become the end goal because we can count them, keep score, and use them to compare ourselves to others. But when we don't look the way we should, or if we don't have the same amount of wealth or abundance of things as others do, we trap ourselves into thinking we are not enough. Such feelings of inadequacy reinforce Adler's theory about seeking power (and money) to overcome our feelings of inferiority. Greed, which is closely related to the pursuit of power, comes in many forms. But in its most fundamental sense, greed stems from fear—the fear of not having enough, of not being successful enough, of not being seen as valuable enough. Greed comes from a perception that we live in a world of scarcity, not abundance, and that survival requires competition over cooperation and collaboration. (Greed, in this context, is an existential phenomenon. It represents yet another sign that something important in life is missing—*meaning*.)

The question is, How much is enough? The costs, both intended and unintended, obvious and hidden, of the hunt for more are staggering. Many of us postpone happiness while we are busy seeking and trying to accumulate more. We ignore our relationships while we focus on amassing more. We overlook our health in our chase for more. Some people spend so much time and energy accruing wealth, only to turn around and spend even more time and energy trying to protect what they've accumulated out of fear that they may lose it. Unfortunately, along with their wealth, they may also lose their "identity." We know that this search for power (through money or otherwise) is parallel to our search for pleasure. This search is external to our real selves, it is "out there." Power over our employees, our bosses, our customers, our shareholders, our kids, the waitress in a restaurant, or a clerk in a retail store is illusory at best and terribly destructive at worst. We think we might have power, but we never know for sure. Even if we do, in the power game there is always an opponent. There is always someone waiting in the wings; the ground is always shifting. Power-seeking is an exhausting game to play. Like pleasure, power is fleeting and always subject to unforeseen forces.

Viktor Frankl believed that the key motivator or driver of human thoughts and actions is the *will to meaning*, not the will to power. Because of this fundamental disagreement, Adler and his protégé Frankl were forced to go their separate ways. Although Frankl learned a great deal from his mentors Freud and Adler, he followed his own path. With an explicit focus on and a dedication to advancing the human quest for meaning, the seeds of Frankl's lifework and legacy had been planted.

Cry for Meaning

In his many lectures and speeches, and in a book first published in 1978, Viktor Frankl passionately warned about an "unheard cry for meaning." He characterized this cry as coming from a combination of depression, aggression, and addiction. These societal symptoms form what Frankl called a "mass neurotic triad." This cry needs to be understood in the context of the underlying existential void. This collective cry is perhaps more prevalent today than when Frankl first identified it, and it doesn't seem to be going away any time soon.

Many Americans are surrounded by more material wealth than any other society in the world. Yet we are restless, unhappy, and disconnected, both from others and from our inner lives. Suicide rates for young people are increasing, and the divide between those with wealth and those on the economic margins is growing. The state of the economy notwithstanding, we have the resources necessary for widespread health care and economic stability, as well as for dealing with the discrepancies between rich and poor, yet the value placed on money for its own sake is taking the place of respect for one another in particular and for humanity in general.

> The truth is that as the struggle for survival has subsided, the question has emerged: survival for what? Even more people today have the means to live but no meaning to live for.[3] (V. Frankl)

Throughout his work Frankl observed that when we are not preoccupied with physical survival, the question turns to *survival for what?* Even as more people today have the financial means to live, they are struggling with the question, What are we living for? In the face of material abundance, our inner emptiness, or "existential vacuum" in Frankl's words, has become ever more pressing. To Frankl, both Freud's will to pleasure and Adler's will to power were manifestations of something missing. In effect, the need or drive to seek pleasure à la Freud and the relentless pursuit of power à la Adler were really just attempts to cover up—not fill—a void of meaning in individuals' lives. Because their will to meaning had been frustrated, for whatever reason, they chose alternative paths to follow—paths based on the premise that pleasure or power (or both) would be able to replace what had been missing.

When people feel empty inside, they turn outward. They look for comfort in pleasure and material things. They look for reassurance in power and trying to control others and the things around them. They think, *If only I can find pleasure or control things, I will find meaning in my life.* They are, unfortunately, mistaken.

Will to Meaning

The will to meaning comes from *within*. Only we can find it, control it, and fulfill it for ourselves. This meaning can sustain us throughout our lives, no matter how little or how much power and pleasure come our way. Most important, meaning sustains us through any pain and suffering we must endure. In his book *Full Catastrophe Living*, mindfulness expert Jon Kabat-Zinn writes about staying connected to our original wholeness no matter what challenges to our health, well-being, and welfare we face. The book explores the lives of those for whom life-threatening illness became a transforming experience. These individuals connected to others in a way that anchored them in love, acceptance, and forgiveness, but they also connected to themselves. Some survived and triumphed over illness, while others didn't. Despite their various challenges, each of these individuals deepened their experience in ways that honored meaning in their life as well as in their death.

When we take the time to cultivate our relationship to our original self, all of our experience becomes grounded in meaning. This was true for Frankl when he observed the behavior of those alongside him imprisoned in the Nazi concentration camps, it was true for those people interviewed in Kabat-Zinn's book, and it is true for anyone who has survived tragedy and allowed their grief to break open their heart to tenderness. When tenderness prevails, we love and forgive ourselves and others. When the opposite happens, when bitterness seals the heart shut, we are isolated from ourselves, from others, and ultimately from meaning itself.

Many of us know someone who has survived tragedy yet somehow retained deep cheerfulness and optimism as the way through life. Charlotte, not long ago, lost a twenty-one-year-old son who had autism. Charlotte candidly described the experience of raising an autistic child, noting that it was not always easy for her or her husband over so many years. On several occasions she recalled reading Frankl's book *Man's Search for Meaning*, underscoring its influence on her thinking and her actions during some of the most difficult moments. Charlotte was able to find deeper meaning in her experience as a parent, no matter how difficult the challenges were, and she learned much about her own humanness through her relationship with her disabled son. When he died suddenly at such a young age, it became clear to Charlotte that his life and legacy would be the ground out of which the rest of her life would be shaped. Significantly, her life has become one shaped by love, generosity, meaningful work, and social activism.

Labyrinths of Meaning

The labyrinth is an analogy for life. It is not a maze or a puzzle to be solved but a path of meaning to be experienced. A labyrinth's path is circular and convoluted, but it has no dead ends. The center is there, but the path takes us through countless twists and turns. We are never really lost, but we can never quite see where we are going. Importantly, we must believe that we are always on the right path. Indeed, there are no wrong paths since every step we take, every experience, teaches us something about our life. Every step has meaning. Along the path we sometimes move forward with ease and confidence, sometimes we cautiously creep ahead, sometimes we find the need to stop and reflect, and other times we feel the urge to retreat. It is a sacred path of individuality, and no one can walk it but oneself.

Perhaps because of my (Alex) Greek family heritage, which is rooted in Crete, I've long been fascinated with the Cretan labyrinth, dating back more than four thousand years. As a child, I was enthralled with the ancient myth of Theseus entering the labyrinth at Knossos to fight the Minotaur. The myth captured my imagination, and I too wanted to explore the unknown. I defied authority to find my own way along the twists and turns of my path. And as convoluted as it sometimes was, the path has remained my own. As I reflect back, there is a harmony in my labyrinth of life that I couldn't have predicted. Somehow, throughout my own journey, I was always guided to find the deeper meaning in what I was experiencing and to anticipate finding meaning in what lay ahead.

In an episode of the popular American TV sitcom *Frasier*, the central character, Dr. Frasier Crane, played by Kelsey Grammer, is notified that he will receive a Lifetime Achievement Award for his work as a psychiatrist and a radio talk show host. Frasier feels ambivalent and even a little depressed about receiving the award. His acceptance speech is noticeably brief and ends with the existential question: "Now what do I do with the rest of my life?" Having been recognized as reaching the pinnacle of his career, he cannot see what he can do to top this award or even where he is supposed to go next. Frasier is fighting the idea that his life is a continuous journey through a labyrinth with all its twists and turns. There is always more to explore, learn, and experience. Drawing upon the wisdom of the ancient Greek philosopher Heraclitus, Frasier needs to be aware that what looks like an *end point* can also be a *beginning point*. Indeed, in so many ways the labyrinth is like life.

Finding this connection in the labyrinth of the work world is not always easy. Everyone, to some degree, wants to feel the connection between their inner world—their true thoughts, feelings, and core beliefs—and their actual work. Tom Chappell, cofounder with his wife, Kate, of the company Tom's of Maine, is a good example of a person who has walked the labyrinth of meaning to find this connection as he navigated the twists and turns of building the company. Tom's journey was guided by his continual search to understand and apply his core beliefs, along with his dedication to always finding the deeper meaning of every challenge.

Indeed, his journey was a true manifestation of realizing the will to meaning.

In the 1960s and 1970s, at the beginning of the American environmental movement, Tom Chappell was concerned about the chemical runoff from cleaning products compromising the health of the soil and ultimately the groundwater systems, oceans, and lakes. In response, he developed Clearlake, a nonphosphate liquid laundry detergent that was environmentally friendly in both product and packaging. Tom expanded his product line to include Tom's of Maine toothpaste, an all-natural product that, unlike other toothpastes then, did not contain sugar. Most supermarkets did not have a natural foods or products section at the time, so Tom's products were sold only through health-food stores. Tom's of Maine products flourished, and the line grew to include mouthwash, deodorants, soap, shampoo, shaving cream, among other products—all made with natural ingredients in environmentally friendly packaging.

Tom had taken his core beliefs about the environment and human health and applied them directly to his business. Despite tremendous success, however, Tom grappled with the meaning of his company and the direction it should take. How could the company adhere to its environmental ethos when there was pressure to increase profits? Should he focus Tom's of Maine on generating more profit, or should he base the company's success on what he could achieve with the profits? Should he alter the products, such as adding saccharin to his toothpaste, to make it more palatable to the mainstream market?

Tom's labyrinth of meaning required heavy doses of ethical and personal decision making. His original vision of the commitment to natural products faced potential compromise by the emphasis on company growth and profits. More troubling, though: Tom no longer felt deeply connected to the company. He questioned whether his core beliefs and values were still reflected in the company he and his wife had founded. Tom's personal journey had started with clean clothes, safe soil, and natural toothpaste, yet now it took him inward. He searched for inspiration. Tom felt called by the Episcopal ministry and considered leaving the company for the seminary. In 1988 he enrolled on a part-time basis at Harvard Divinity School. For the next three years, Tom spent two-and-a-half days a week in Kennebunk, Maine, running the company, and the remainder of the week at school in Cambridge, Massachusetts. At Harvard he studied the writings of the great moral and religious philosophers and tried to relate their ideas to business in general and to Tom's of Maine in particular.

He was influenced by the work of Martin Buber, the twentieth-century Jewish philosopher who espoused that there are two opposite types of relationships we can have with others. In the I-It relationship we treat other people as objects and expect something back from each relationship. In contrast, in the I–Thou relationship we relate to others out of respect, friendship, and love. In other words, we either see others as objects to use for our selfish purposes or we honor people for their own sake. Tom recognized that he and Kate instinctively operated their company using the I–Thou relationship, but unfortunately many of his new managers were following the I-It model. He was also deeply influenced by the writings of the eighteenth-century American philosopher Jonathan Edwards, who believed that an individual's true identity comes not from being separate but from being in relationship with others. As Tom applied this thinking to his company, he realized that the relationships with employees, suppliers, customers, financial partners, governments, communities, and even the Earth itself were what shaped the company's true identity.

With his fresh insights, Tom returned full-time to lead Tom's of Maine. His vision of the company as a social and moral entity as well as a business organization more deeply reflected Tom's spiritual beliefs, which reinforced his connection to the outside world. The business continued to be a success in the broadest possible terms—satisfying Tom's personal spiritual yearnings and will to meaning as well as strengthening the bottom line. When Tom based his company's development on meaningful goals, he brought deep personal meaning to his own life. In short, it is a partnership of meaning. Tom's of Maine, founded on Chappell's youthful ideals, effectively became his ministry. Following the ideals of Viktor Frankl, the business can be described as a ministry of meaning.[4]

Going Within

We cannot wait for solutions magically to arrive; rather, we have to actively be a part of the solution to whatever problems or challenges we face. Former NBA coach Phil Jackson, in his book *Sacred Hoops*, cautions us to remember that the best way to realize one's dreams is to wake up! Being part of any solution means taking action. And taking action involves more than just dreaming, no matter how vivid, how real, one's dreams appear. Whether dreaming or awake, when we are prisoners of our thoughts, we can't always see very clearly through the bars of our metaphorical prison cell, let alone take action. To see more clearly, we must be willing to go inward:

> It's time to go inward, take a look at myself.
> Time to make the most of the time that I've got left.
> Prison bars imagined are no less solid steel.[5]

Once again, we are reminded of the many twists and turns that occur naturally, although not always seamlessly, as we explore the labyrinth of meaning in our personal and work lives. Exploring the labyrinth involves a willingness and an authentic commitment to embark down a path of *self-discovery* and realize what Viktor Frankl referred to as our will to meaning—that is, our inherent capacity to continually search for meaning under *all* circumstances.

> Unconditional meaning, however, is paralleled by the unconditional value of each and every person. It is that which warrants the indelible quality of the dignity of man. Just as life remains potentially meaningful under any conditions, even those which are most miserable, so too does the value of each and every person stay with him or her.[6] (V. Frankl)

Unfortunately, we frequently miss opportunities to enjoy the spaciousness that already exists *within* us to feel authentic meaning in our lives and work. Frankl would argue that only if we remain aware of and committed to meaningful values and goals will we be able to fully enjoy this spaciousness. To be sure, the most difficult thing in life is to know ourselves. It takes time and effort to question, reflect, and know authentically who we are—not what others want us to be. It takes time and effort to know our strengths and talents and use them in service to others. It takes time and effort to understand what brings meaning to our lives. This quest for meaning requires that we accept the challenge of the labyrinth and venture within.

As the ancient Greek philosopher Socrates wisely advised, we should *go within* and listen to our inner voice. We should trust our inner voice and not be swayed by others. Through observation, questioning, logic, and an understanding of metaphysics (the nature of existence beyond the physical), we can sharpen our perspectives and gain greater awareness of ourselves. Socrates was famous for suggesting that "the unexamined life is not worth living." Steve Jobs, the cofounder of Apple, so appreciated these ageless words of wisdom that he once professed: "I would trade all my technology for an afternoon with Socrates."[7] In the final analysis, it is the ability to go within and to realize our will to meaning—our authentic commitment to meaningful values and goals that only we can actualize and fulfill—that guides us in the quest to tap into our uniqueness as human beings and achieve our full potential in life and work.

In the vast exploration of our inner and outer lives, Frankl's will to meaning rises above and distinguishes itself from the will to pleasure and the will to power. Only we can find it, control it, and fulfill it for ourselves. It is *meaning* that sustains us throughout our lives, no matter how little or how much power and pleasure come our way. It is *meaning* that waits to be discovered by us and for us, but it can only happen if we choose *not* to be prisoners of our thoughts.

Meaning Reflections

The "Mountain Range Exercise" is based on Frankl's invitation, in his book *The Doctor and the Soul,* to spread our lives out before us like a beautiful mountain range. See your life (or specifically, your work life) as a landscape with mountains and valleys. What are the events and who are the people who most influenced you? Put these on the mountain peaks. What are the events and who are the people who most dissuaded you or even disrespected you? Put these in the valleys. Now review and look for patterns in the names on the mountain peaks. What is most meaningful about these people or events? What are the recurring themes and values that were communicated? How did you learn from and incorporate these themes and values into your life? Now look for recurring themes and values in the valleys of your life. What did you learn from these experiences or people? This "Mountain Range Exercise" helps you look at your personal and work life from a different perspective. Through it you can discover recurring values, recognize your own uniqueness, and broaden your view about your work and personal life. It is an unfolding exercise, a new way of discovering your will to meaning in life and work.

Meaning Questions

- Which drives your thoughts and actions in your personal life the most: the will to pleasure, the will to power (including the accumulation of money), or the will to meaning?
- In what ways is your life a journey through a labyrinth?

- How do you remain committed to meaningful values and goals and thereby realize your will to meaning in your personal and work life?

Meaning Affirmation

I will focus on the goal of realizing the will to meaning versus focusing on pleasure or power.

PRINCIPLE 3. Detect the Meaning of Life's Moments

Live as if you were living already for the second time
and as if you had acted the first time as wrongly
as you are about to act now![1] (V. Frankl)

It is not the meaning of life per se that is important; rather, it is the search for meaning in *your own life* that is important. Meaning is different for everyone—there is no one right answer; there is only the answer that is right for you. However, the search for meaning in our own lives often seems like such a large undertaking. Where do we begin? Making this task more manageable is the subject of this chapter in which we introduce the third principle of Frankl's work: detecting the meaning of life's moments.

FINDING MEANING

We don't create meaning—we *find* it. And we can't find it if we don't look for it. Sometimes it looms large in our lives; sometimes it slips in almost unobserved. We might miss a meaningful moment entirely, until days, months, or even years later when what once seemed insignificant is revealed as a pivotal, life-changing moment. Or it might be the collective meaning of many moments that finally catches our mind's eye, as if we weave together a living quilt from moments that by themselves passed unnoticed. Although we are not always aware of meaning, Frankl would say that it is present in *every* moment, wherever we go. All we have to do, in daily life and at work, is to wake up to meaning and take notice:

> *The true meaning of life is to be discovered in the world rather than within man or his own psyche, as if it were a closed system.*[2]
> (V. Frankl)

We cannot answer the big question about the meaning of our own life unless we discover answers to the smaller ones: What are we doing? Why are we doing it? What does this relationship mean? What does our work mean? Every day our lives are rich with meaningful answers, but only when we stop long enough to appreciate meaning will it bloom in our lives. We have to be in touch to detect and know meaning, but most of the time we are on our way somewhere else, caught up in the frenzy of work or personal challenges. If we don't stop to search out and be mindful of our own existence, meaning will recede to an impossible dream. Our entire lives are rich with meaning, and therefore everything we do has meaning. We are free to make decisions out of love for whatever is in our hearts. When we stop to look at the reasons for our decisions, we will find meaning. Taking time to reflect on the meaning of each of life's moments is the first step to opening ourselves to the deeper overall meaning of our individual lives.

Unfortunately, not everyone takes the time or makes the effort to find meaning in life's moments. Take Michelle, for example, who had recently celebrated her fiftieth birthday but was not quite ready to admit that she had reached the half-century mark. She was dreading facing her journey into the next few decades, including retirement. She was not happy and not inclined to celebrate anything in her life. Twice divorced and the single mother of two Generation Xers, Michelle felt that her personal life left much to be desired. Her work life was unsatisfying as well. Since her last marriage had ended, Michelle had been unable to hold any kind of steady employment. Whenever she did find a worthwhile job, it seemed to sour quickly. Over and over, Michelle found herself stressed at work, for some reason that had nothing to do with herself—a poor boss, lazy coworkers, an unclear job description, lack of support, and so on. Consequently, she was never satisfied with her work situation. She never imagined that she could find meaningful work.

At work and at home Michelle was consumed by a need to put out fires, leaving little in reserve for determining the root causes of her suffering. As she grew increasingly depressed over her life situation, Michelle externalized the reasons for her plight, which hardened into a fixed habit. Oblivious to her own role and responsibility as co-creator of her miserable reality, she effectively had lost touch with the meaning of life's precious moments because she was too busy complaining about what life was doing *to* her. In her mind, life had dealt her a bad hand, so there was nothing to do but bear the suffering and complain loudly enough so everyone around her—family, friends, coworkers—would hear her cries of anguish. "The meaning of it all is that there is no meaning," said the golfer Walter Hogan in the movie *The Legend of Bagger Vance*. Michelle would agree with this statement, for the search for meaning had no value to her. Her life seemed meaningless and would continue to seem meaningless—unless some sort of miracle came her way. By giving up on her search for meaning, Michelle had chosen to take an early retirement from life.

In contrast, let's consider Adam, who wrote to us after reading an earlier edition of *Prisoners of Our Thoughts* and applying the book's principles in response to a major life and work transition. After thirty years as a corporate engineer, Adam found himself being transferred from a position he loved and moving to another area of the organization that literally had no work for him. The organization was undergoing many changes, and Adam feared that the move was simply a step toward being laid off, a step toward the door. Suddenly, his life had no meaning, and he suffered through months of self-pitying thoughts that held him prisoner. After reading the book, he began to look at his situation as an opportunity rather than a problem. As a result, Adam began to reinvent himself. Although he could not immediately change his circumstances, he could change his attitude toward how he perceived the situation. He could find a deeper meaning in it.

Gradually, as Adam's attitude improved, so did his disposition, his outlook on life and work, and his progress toward a completely new type of personal fulfillment and professional success. He attributed much of this change in perspective and behavior to his newly found appreciation for the potential for meaning that exists in *all* of life's moments, even those that are not particularly pleasant, welcomed, or expected. Adam realized that his former "poor me" thoughts would not resolve his predicament, and that he alone was responsible for discovering the seeds of meaning that existed in his life. Unlike Michelle, Adam assumed full responsibility for his situation, and he refused to take an early retirement from life by giving up on his search for meaning.

To find authentic meaning in our lives, we need courage, which is not the absence of fear but the willingness and ability to walk *through* the fear—to tread, if you will, into the darkness of life's labyrinth of meaning. It is during the worst times, through hardship and suffering, that our courage is put to its greatest test. Consider the film *Defending Your Life* in which director/writer Albert Brooks plays Dan Miller, a successful business executive who delights in taking delivery of a brand-new BMW. Just as he is pulling out of the car dealership, he has the misfortune of crashing into a bus. Dan does not survive the accident and finds himself in the afterlife, in a heavenly way station called Judgment City. Here, Dan discovers that he must stand trial and justify his life in order to either advance to the next, higher plane of existence or be sent back to earth to repeat his life.

In a courtroom Dan is shown video clips of his life and asked to defend his actions, especially when fear was most evident. Here is a sample of the dialogue between Dan and his defense attorney, Bob Diamond (played by actor Rip Torn):

> BOB DIAMOND: Being from earth as you are and using as little of your brain as you do, your life has pretty much been devoted to dealing with fear.

DAN MILLER: It has?

BOB DIAMOND: Everybody on earth deals with fear. That's what little brains do.

. . .

BOB DIAMOND: Did you ever have friends whose stomachs hurt?

DAN MILLER: Every one of them.

BOB DIAMOND: It's fear. Fear is like a giant fog. It sits on your brain and blocks everything. Real feeling, true happiness, real joy, they can't get through that fog. But you lift it and, buddy, you're in for the ride of your life.

As the Bob Diamond character explains, most people only use 3 to 5 percent of their brain's potential, limiting themselves because of their fears. They can't see past their fears, nor can they see the deeper meaning in the small moments of their lives, which robs them of experiencing the beauty and fullness of life. Many of us can relate to Dan Miller's character and might even wonder what video clips would be shown at our own trial should we end up in Judgment City, having to defend our life!

Many people don't want to explore the meaning of situations in which they find themselves, as shown in the example of Michelle and in Dan Miller's character. More often than not, people fear what they might uncover, what they might have to address. They simply "can't go there." Many people do not want to confront their weaknesses, choosing instead to ignore them or, worse yet, to blame others. Some people choose to busy themselves with activities and diversions so that they don't have to slow down and actually look at their own lives. Others simply don't know what steps they should take to find this deeper meaning.

Existential Digging

As we've already mentioned, we can't find meaning, even when surrounded by it, unless we look for it. Our "Existential Digging Exercise" provides an easy way to detect the meaning of life's moments. Whenever you encounter an experience or situation that is especially challenging, or one that you would describe as a meaning moment in your personal or work life, ask yourself these questions:

1. How did you *respond* to the situation or life experience? What did you do and think?

2. How did you *feel* about the situation or life experience? What kinds of emotions were stirred up as a result of the experience or situation?

3. What did you *learn* from the situation or life experience? What new knowledge, skills, or attitude do you now possess because of the experience or situation?

4. How will you *grow* from the situation or life experience? How will you apply what you have learned from the experience or situation, especially key learning about yourself, for your personal development?

Dig deep for the insights from your experience. Review how you *responded*, how you *felt*, what you *learned*, and, most important, how you will *grow* from this experience.

By faithfully and authentically addressing these four levels of existential questions, we guarantee that you will engage in the systematic process of detecting the meaning of life's moments. Obviously you cannot respond to the four questions for every moment of your life, but we highly recommend that you try to address situations or life experiences that really matter—or should matter—in your personal life and work life. These may be those moments that are (or were) especially positive, negative, challenging, and/or stressful for you. We also suggest that you maintain a journal or some other kind of record or diary so that you can periodically review your experiences and chart your progress in dealing with the meaning of life's moments. Are you really growing and developing as a result of your learning from various life situations, or are you simply repeating old patterns of thinking and behavior? Do you recognize any common threads of meaning that may help you weave your unique tapestry of existence?

The Importance of Awareness

Everything comes down to awareness. It has been said that "it is more important to be aware than it is to be smart."[3] To be aware is to know meaning. To be aware takes time and effort. If our lives are dominated by too many activities or passive preoccupation with television, our smartphones, or the Internet, we lose out on the meaning that surrounds us. We must be aware—see, hear, smell, touch, and taste the world—to find the meaning in our lives.

> All that is good and beautiful in the past is safely preserved in that past. On the other hand, so long as life remains, all guilt and all evil are still "redeemable." . . . This is not the case of a finished

film . . . or an already existent film that is merely being unrolled. Rather, the film of this world is just being "shot." Which means nothing more or less than that the future—happily—still remains to be shaped; that is, it is at the disposal of man's responsibility.[4]
(V. Frankl)

There are as many shades of meaning as there are colors. Nobody can determine meaning for someone else—detecting the meaning of life's moments is an individual's personal responsibility. Like it or not, if we are aware that we're in a lousy job but we need to pay the rent, the job still has meaning. We needn't resign ourselves to a lifelong lousy job, but there is meaning in the one we have right now. We just need to look for the meaning. If we dislike our boss because he or she is demanding and unappreciative, we can either be demanding and unappreciative right back or try to discover a life lesson in our predicament. Maybe the boss is trying too hard to succeed; maybe we're hearing a parental voice from our past rather than that of the boss; maybe we have an opportunity to practice our diplomatic skills with a difficult person. Or perhaps we are in a job that is not right for us!

In *Man's Search for Meaning*, Viktor Frankl describes a case in which he met with a high-ranking American diplomat at his office in Vienna, presumably to continue psychoanalytic treatment that this person had begun five years earlier in New York City.[5] At the outset Dr. Frankl asked the diplomat why he thought that he should undergo analysis—why it had started in the first place? It turned out that this patient had been discontent with his career and had found it difficult to comply with American foreign policy. His former analyst, however, had told him again and again that he should to try to reconcile himself with his father, because his employer (the U.S. government) and his superiors were nothing but father figures. Consequently, according to this analyst's line of thinking, his dissatisfaction with his job was a result of hatred he unconsciously harbored toward his father.

For five years the diplomat had accepted this interpretation of his plight, and he became increasingly confused— unable to see the forest of reality for the trees of symbols and images. After a few interviews with Dr. Frankl, it was clear that the diplomat's real problem was not a hatred for his father but that he longed to be engaged in another kind of work. In essence, his will to meaning was being frustrated. As a result of this insight, the diplomat decided to give up his profession and embark on another one, which, as it turned out, proved to be very gratifying. His anguish had been not because of his father but because of his own inability to choose work that had true meaning for him. As this example shows, if we allow ourselves to be aware of the many possibilities open to us, we open ourselves to meaning.

The more aware we are, the more likely we can start to see the patterns in our thoughts, words, and behaviors. We can start to see patterns in how we deal with work challenges. We can start to see patterns in how we deal with relationships. Through this connection we may come to realize that we are attracting the same kind of personal or romantic relationships over and over again, relationships that might be negative or even toxic and therefore not serving our highest good. We may come to realize that we have a habit of wanting to lash out at others or take revenge if they demand too much of us. We may realize that we only like to look at *our* side of the story instead of realizing that there are many sides to the same story. The more aware we are, the more likely we'll begin to see patterns in how we approach our health. We may realize that we are not expressing our emotions, bottling up our anger, which leads to more stress. We may realize that our weight gain may be a result of stress and not specifically to do with the chocolate cake we ate last week!

The more we become aware of the moments in our life, the more we open ourselves to meaning. Many people define "meaning" as "significance" or "something that matters." However, we define meaning as "resonance with our true nature or core essence." When something feels significant, when we know that it matters, it is because it resonates with whom we truly are. For example, I (Elaine) traveled many times to the small villages of Greece and witnessed how the villagers live so simply and find great meaning in interacting with each other. I thought of all the "stuff" I had at home in America and wondered why I needed so much. As I reflected on these moments, my awareness grew. It wasn't a question of being materialistic or antimaterialistic; it was a question of what role money and things should play in my life. I concluded that the ultimate goal was to find *inner* prosperity first and then layer on any materialism, as opposed to starting the other way round—embracing materialism and hoping one day to find meaning. Upon returning from one of these journeys, I decided to downsize, to unload some of the stuff with which I had surrounded myself. I chose, instead, to focus my journey on meaning. This meaning moment or meaning experience taught me to seek greater awareness and to live in a way that resonates with who I believe I am at the core.

It is life itself that invites us to discover meaning, and when we live with awareness, we express meaning in everything we do. *Webster's New International Dictionary* lists more than twenty definitions for the word *work* and more than a hundred other terms or phrases that begin with the word *work*. But it's the first definition, with its two small root words—*to do*—that illustrates the meaning of them all. Whatever we *do* has meaning, whether it's a workout or a work of art.

Life retains its meaning under any conditions. It remains meaningful literally up to its last moment, up to one's last breath.[6]
(V. Frankl)

Knowing *why* we do things, however, is essential and is the beginning of real freedom and meaning in our lives. If we delve deep enough, we'll reach the two things that motivate us most: love and conscience. Frankl described these as intuitive capabilities: things we do without thinking, things that define us at our deepest level. "The truth," he wrote in *Man's Search for Meaning*, "is that love is the ultimate and the highest goal to which man can aspire."

It's not always easy to trace where love and conscience come into play in our lives, but if we explore our decisions, they surface: We work nights so we can be with our kids in the morning and see them off to school. We grow vegetables organically to provide healthy food for the community. We operate a small business that offers employment to three people year-round in a difficult economy. We write poems to encourage family and friends. We consult with others to help them cope with stress. We teach sailing to inner-city kids.

We manage a corporation with an emphasis on fair wages for workers abroad. We make quilts for families who are homeless. We work at a job we don't love because it gives us money to do something we do love. We organize fundraisers to bring affordable housing to our community. We donate a thousand dollars to a local charity. We put a dollar in an outstretched hand. We build energy-efficient straw-bale houses. We wait tables so we can be onstage, raise our kids, feed our dog, or pay the light bill. It all comes down to love and conscience. When we see how our world is connected in this way, we can name the *why* and know deeper meaning.

Drafting Our Legacy

As your awareness grows, you can start to see patterns in the meaning in each moment. You can string together these insights to see the bigger picture of your life. You can see all of the roads you have taken, all of the stops you have made, all of the people you have encountered, all of the things you have done or experienced in your life. What are the most important, most meaningful things you have experienced? You can also project or envision what your life may be like in the future. Think about your life—past, present, and future. Now imagine if you were, say, a hundred years old, and you looked back at your entire life. What would you see? What did you accomplish? What impact did you have on others? In other words, what was your *legacy*? The most common definition of the word *legacy*, sadly, is "a gift of money or property, usually left to someone in a will." When we refer to *legacy*, we are not referring to money. Rather, we are referring to something that is passed on from generation to generation—a lesson, an impact, a story, some wisdom—that enables a person's life, in effect, to "live on" eternally.

Our powerful "Eulogy Exercise" is shown in Figure 1. A eulogy is a speech or writing in praise of a person or thing, especially someone who has recently died. Since you will be writing your own eulogy, the objective of this exercise is for you to reflect on the meaning of the moments of your life and to determine how you would like to be remembered. What was important about your life, and what impact did you have on others? How did you make a difference in this world? In this exercise, fill in the blanks on the form and make sure that these final comments about you, to be recited at your funeral, are really what you want said![7] This unique opportunity allows you to write your own eulogy, so make sure that you incorporate the things that matter most to you. Did you live and work with meaning? Now assume that someone else wrote your eulogy. What would be different? Would others say the same things about you and your impact? Would others say that you lived and worked with meaning?

Reflecting on your life and work through this exercise, you are able to detect what is most meaningful to you. The "Eulogy Exercise" asks you to see the big picture of your life, albeit still as a work in progress. You may or may not like what you see. Yet this exercise offers you the chance to consider your life's *ultimate* meaning, as Frankl would say. Whatever your religious or spiritual beliefs are, *ultimate meaning* is a metaphysical concept that has its roots and values in spiritual

Eulogy Exercise

Are you living and working in such a way that the last comments about you, especially from your family, friends, business associates, and customers/clients, are really what you want to have said? Imagine now that you have passed on and have been given the opportunity to write your own eulogy to be read at your funeral. Go ahead, fill in the blanks!

We have gathered here today to say farewell to _____. The world had a great need for someone who _____ _____ and _____ was the right person to fulfill this need.

_____ was most fulfilled when _____ _____ _____.

I believe _____ was put on this earth to _____ _____ _____.

The world is a much better place because _____ was here and we will miss her/him forever.

Figure 1. Eulogy Exercise.

matters. In his introduction to *The Doctor and the Soul*, Dr. Frankl wrote: "Life is a task. The religious man differs from the apparently irreligious man only by experiencing his existence not simply as a task, but as a mission." Viewing life as inherently meaningful and with unlimited potential requires a shift in consciousness. It requires responsible action on our part for, as Frankl pointed out, the potential for meaning that exists in each moment of life can only be searched for and detected by each of us individually. This responsibility, he wrote, is "to be actualized by each of us at any time, even in the most miserable situations and literally up to the last breath of ourselves."[8] By remaining aware of the need to detect and learn from the meaning of life's moments, we ensure that we do not become prisoners of our thoughts. By focusing on meaning's big picture, while simultaneously seeking to notice life's meaning moments, our search for ultimate meaning begins and never ends.

Meaning Reflections

Meaning Moment Exercise — Imagine that you have written your autobiography—with details about your life and work—and it is now on the *New York Times* best-seller list. What is the title of your autobiography? Name and briefly describe the chapters in your autobiography. Who are the people included in your acknowledgments?

- What is the meaning you are detecting from reading this book?
- What type of existential digging do you do to unearth the meaning of life's moments?
- How is your life or work like a mission versus just a series of tasks?

Meaning Affirmation

I will look for and find meaning in the various experiences of my life.

PRINCIPLE 4.
Don't Work Against Yourself

Ironically enough, in the same way that fear brings to pass what one is afraid of, likewise a forced intention makes impossible what one forcibly wishes.[1] (V. Frankl)

Have you ever worked so hard at something that the more you tried, the harder the task became and the farther away you seemed to get from your goal? In other words, one step forward, two steps back? I (Alex) have experienced this kind of situation in my life, especially in my work life. Let me share an example that took place when I was a full-time professor, directing a graduate degree program in public administration at a university in the United States. Among my duties as director, I was charged with the challenge of obtaining accreditation for the program from a professional association. Becoming accredited was viewed by those in the field as a prestigious distinction and competitive advantage, through which my program stood to gain increases in student enrollment and research funding, greater ease of faculty recruitment, and other embellishments for its resource base.

As a new faculty member, I took on the responsibility of seeking this accreditation milestone as a way of making my mark. I moved full-steam ahead, demonstrating that I was committed and passionate, convinced that the objective would be reached in short order. I had been through this same accreditation process before at other institutions, which I felt was sufficient evidence that I knew what I was doing. My experience would carry me through to another victory. Alas, this did not turn out to be the case. I found pockets of resistance everywhere I looked, and the more I looked, the more resistance I found. My expertise in this process, I learned later, proved to be a liability. I thought I knew what to do. I thought I knew how to do it *best*. I thought all of my colleagues were doing it wrong! I became fixated on every detail of the program, and I assured myself that single-handedly I would be able to correct any and all imperfections that might jeopardize the objective of gaining full accreditation.

I had good intentions, and in hindsight most of my university colleagues would probably agree with me. Unfortunately, my fixation on the outcome backfired, and I was unable to fulfill the ultimate goal. I never was able to obtain accreditation during my tenure as program head. I could easily blame the situation on everyone else or at least shift the bulk of responsibility for failing to reach my objective onto others. I choose not to, however, for I can see how my own actions worked against me. I tried too hard to get everything done my way and, as a result, estranged myself from the very colleagues upon whom I depended for success. My fixation on the "right" way to do things marginalized the contributions of my colleagues and, in some cases, invited forms of subtle— if not overt—sabotage. I had become my own worst enemy, and at the time I didn't even know it!

The meaning of life is meaning. The meaning of life *at work* is meaning. When we look for meaning, there is meaning in the looking. It's right here, all around us, within us, and beyond us. But if we try too hard to create meaning, it can backfire, especially at work. Like our personal lives, our jobs come complete with their own dynamics. But unlike in our personal relationships, we can't always interact with our coworkers with emotional honesty and vulnerability. We are often afraid to confront others, to tell them what we are really thinking, for fear of reprisal. We shy away from conflict in order to appear professional. We tell ourselves to focus on the task at hand, to ignore the human dynamics.

> *Work usually represents the area in which the individual's uniqueness stands in relation to society and thus acquires meaning and value. This meaning and value, however, is attached to the person's work as a contribution to society, not to the actual occupation as such.*[2] (V. Frankl)

Most often our performance on the job is measurable— what we produce might be immediately tangible: making sales or products, meeting a quota, driving a certain distance in a day, meeting a deadline, baking bread, fixing a car, or serving a customer, for example. Other professional responsibilities are less tangible: involving long-term planning and projects that require creative involvement, teamwork, complex expectations, and more subjective goal-setting. They all require performance and most often evaluation as well. Most of us are accountable to others in our jobs. We want to please, to perform well, and to be effective at what we do. Often, when we most want to impress others, we undermine ourselves. We become obsessed with results, and we overlook the very success we are seeking.

Relationships at Work

One reason we may miss succeeding is that we overlook the importance of relationships in the workplace. Our jobs are always more than just jobs. They represent relationships—with coworkers and ourselves; with customers and consumers; with the products we are designing, creating, and selling; with the services we offer; and with the environment and the ways in which our work affects the world. These relationships weave together through our work, and they have meaning individually and collectively. When we focus too intently on outcomes, these relationships suffer. The harder we work for success, the more elusive it can become.

> *The job at which one works is not what counts, but rather the manner in which one does the work.*[3] (V. Frankl)

Consider Angela's experience. Angela had just graduated from college with a degree in business administration, and she was especially excited when she was promoted to a supervisory position at the drugstore where she worked. It was her first attempt at being a manager, and she envisioned this promotion as her initial step up the corporate ladder. Of course, Angela wanted more than anything to do her best in the new job and prove to her bosses that they made the right decision in promoting her. Right away, she proclaimed her intentions for building better teamwork, sharing responsibilities, and improving performance with all the employees on her shift. Angela's enthusiasm appeared to be contagious, and it looked as if she would immediately be able to make some major improvements. However, Angela soon found out that good intentions are not enough.

"My coworkers are unbelievably lazy," she complained to the customers, "and they don't carry their weight around here no matter what I say or do." Indeed, Angela displayed an extremely negative attitude about work and was quick to point out the failings of other employees. Her work situation had become dysfunctional for reasons that were largely her own doing. She had been exhibiting two behavioral traits or tendencies—*hyperintention* and *hyper-reflection*—that are central to Viktor Frankl's teachings. Angela was unaware that she had begun to micromanage her employees in order to attain her goals of demonstrating that she was a good manager and achieving her stated performance objectives. She had become so fixated on accomplishing her mission (that is, *hyperintending*) that she had forsaken the means for the end. Because she was so obsessed with reaching her goals, Angela fixated on the problems that she saw. The more she looked, the more she saw (that is, *hyper-reflecting*). Despite her good intentions, she actually worked against herself by focusing on the problems, not the solutions to her escalating management dilemma.

As a result, the more she complained and called for increased teamwork, job sharing, and improved performance, the less she saw among her coworkers. Angela had become so consumed with her intended outcome—a form of anticipatory anxiety—that she began to see herself failing to achieve it. She became even more negative about the situation and, in effect, had unconsciously created a self-fulfilling prophecy, as many of us do. The more problems she saw, the more problems she had. The more problems she had, the more negative she became. The more negative she became, the less her team wanted to excel. A vicious cycle had begun. Unfortunately, Angela was unaware that letting go of (or at least relaxing) her intentions would probably have allowed her to find ways to resolve the situation and fulfill her original work objectives.

I (Elaine) have also been guilty of hyper-reflection at work. Although I was blessed with leading a group of very skilled managers at a multinational company, one of the managers always seemed to lag behind. I thought the best approach to inspire improvement was to coach him every day, to clearly outline my expectations. However, the more I singled him out, the more I highlighted where his work was below par, the worse he performed. In hindsight, I realize that I was micromanaging this manager's performance when I should have taken the opposite approach—encouraging him and letting him rise to the occasion on his own. Indeed, I learned from this experience that good intentions are not always enough!

We should point out that hyperintention and hyper-reflection, in many ways, are similar to a condition called *hypochondria*, now known as Illness Anxiety Disorder—an obsession with the idea of having a serious or life-threatening but undiagnosed medical condition. Although these people may not actually be ill, the thought of being so and the anticipatory anxiety that is associated with it end up making them sick! In effect, hypochondriacs are working against themselves!

Paradoxical Intention

Meaning is found in the awareness of the moment, and when we move too far from the moment, we start to lose our effectiveness. Even when the stakes are high and our success essential, focusing obsessively on the results rather than on the process can result in failure to achieve our intended aim. We all know how this works: our nervousness and anxiety about getting it right keep us from getting it right. The higher our expectations are about something, the more disconnected we are from the actual process, and the less we are able to participate in the project's successful unfolding. Viktor Frankl calls this *paradoxical intention*. Our good intentions actually become the cause of our failure. When a specific success is so fervently sought that we overlook and neglect the relationships that are an integral part of the process, we lay the seeds for something to go wrong. We fly in the face of our own success. We neglect our own meaning, the meaning of others, and the meaning of the process.

"My boss is a jerk." "My boss hates me." "My boss steals all the credit." How many times have you made or heard statements like these? Think about what you are saying, what it really means, and how it may be affecting you and your coworkers. Bosses do have flaws, but on the whole most people deserve the positions they hold. They have usually moved up in the organization for a good reason. If you dismiss your boss because of her or his flaws, you may be cheating yourself

Principle 4. Don't Work Against Yourself

out of a chance to learn and grow. What is your boss good at? What can you learn from him or her? What kinds of workers get along best with your boss? Are *you* doing anything that brings out the worst in your boss? From the perspective of Frankl's paradoxical intention, are you encouraging your boss to be a micromanager by asking questions every few minutes rather than by doing your job well? You might be working against yourself!

Human beings are intuitive, affected by the moods of those around us; we know feelings of trust and mistrust; we know when something just doesn't feel right. We recognize when we are being treated badly, superficially, carelessly, or dishonestly, whether in our personal life or our work life. We know when we are being used as part of someone else's agenda. We can sense when our intrinsic meaning as a human being is being overlooked in the wake of somebody else's ambition. Something is missing, and it's usually meaning.

Consider Neal, a software engineer at a major high-tech firm. Newly married, Neal had just completed an MBA degree from a prestigious university and was determined to be promoted to a management position as quickly as possible. He was so determined to show off his newly acquired management knowledge and skills—primarily as a way to propel himself up the corporate ladder—that he went out of his way to be noticed by his supervisors, even if it meant ignoring or irritating his coworkers. Neal's technical skills as a software engineer were recognized, but his people skills were not. In fact, his coworkers did not consider him a team player, let alone a supervisor or leader, and they voiced their disdain for him whenever possible. At team meetings, during performance reviews, and in the lunch room, Neal the aspiring manager was targeted by his coworkers as being out of touch. He was disliked by the very colleagues he had hoped to supervise.

Because Neal was so busy looking at his prospects for promotion, he failed to see that the water was beginning to boil all around him. No matter how competent he portrayed himself as a manager, and no matter how hard he tried to convince his bosses to promote him, he was unable to do so. Neal was fixated on the possible promotion, but the more he tried to get it, the farther out of reach it became. Because he was unaware of the meaning moments that begged for his attention, he was unable to adjust his course. Neal was working against himself.

Whenever we overlook the opportunity to have respectful, meaningful moments with others at work, we undermine our chances of long-term success. But when we take the time to nurture our relationships, the definition of success expands exponentially. Our day-to-day, minute-by-minute lives become successful in and of themselves, and our specific goals become more accessible. In work relationships it is important to recognize that business and personal issues are frequently tied together. "Smart companies know that the individual's ability to create relationships" is the engine that drives value.[4] Trusting each other's motives is critical to success, both in the moment and over the long haul. If trust is missing, we can get caught up not only in figuring out how others are trying to undermine us but also in calculating how best to respond to their motivations. As a result, the search for meaning at work suffers, and the engine that drives value sputters or stalls.

The tendency to hold others, such as coworkers, prisoners of our own thoughts can work in ways opposite to our intentions. For example, in their article "The Set-Up-to-Fail Syndrome," Jean-François Manzoni and Jean-Louis Barsoux describe the way bosses often relegate weaker performers to an "out-group" because they assume that these employees are less willing to go the extra mile, are more passive, and are less innovative.[5] This management approach, and the assumptions upon which it is based, becomes a self-fulfilling prophecy. Because these employees have been typecast as weak performers and management has low expectations of them, they tend to allow their performance to erode to meet expectations. So even though the bosses sought to get the best performance possible through the out-group assignment, their personal attitudes and business decisions eventually worked against them. The tendency to micromanage the work of others may create hyperintensive stress, performance anxiety, or even covert or overt actions of sabotage that can end up creating the opposite of the result sought by a manager. (A similar result also has been observed in cases where well-meaning parents, under the guise of parental guidance, try to micromanage their teenagers, who are predisposed to being contrarian!) Sometimes focusing too closely on a problem can keep us from seeing the solution.

The opposite of micromanagers are missing managers, who stay so far out of the picture they have no idea what goes on and have no effect on the success of the work group. There are also those managers who profess to practice management by wandering around (known as MBWA managers): "Keep up the good work, whatever it is, whoever you are!" If the micromanager, the missing manager, and the MBWA manager can instead honor the fact that the job means something to everyone, and that most employees have good intentions, then more success is possible.

> *For the dignity of man forbids his being himself a means, his becoming a mere instrument of the labor process, being degraded to a means of production. The capacity to work is not everything; it is neither a sufficient nor essential basis for a meaningful life. A man can be capable of working and nevertheless not lead a meaningful life; and another can be incapable of working and nevertheless give his life meaning.*[6] (V. Frankl)

Few of us move through our lives unscathed. We get divorced; we lose our jobs, sometimes after many years of dedicated service; our health fails us in some way; our children fail us; we fail one another. Life can be as full of failures as it is successes. Yet in our failures we can find tremendous meaning, and only in meaning do our failures have a useful legacy. When our failures become useful, we triumph over them. Instead of leading with our disappointment and bitterness over a job loss or a lost relationship, we lead with our ability to have compassion and understanding—for ourselves and others. Then, in our search for our next job, our next friend, or better health, we project wisdom and experience. Our appeal is heightened and our possibilities increase. The power of failure has received an increasing amount of attention in the world of business, both in the literature and among motivational speakers.[7] Management guru Tom Peters, for instance, has advised that "only with failure can you verify wrong ways of doing things and discard those practices that hinder success."[8] Tales of failure that offer lessons of recovery are being used by many who are turning to the "drama of defeat" to inspire.

Using Paradoxical Intention

Paradoxical intention is more than a concept; it is a technique that Frankl developed and incorporated into his system of Logotherapy. Frankl used this technique as early as 1939 to help patients deal with a broad range of irrational fears and anxieties as well as obsessive-compulsive behaviors. For example, by asking a patient who suffered from a phobia to *intend*, even if only for a moment, precisely that which he or she feared, Frankl observed dramatic results in reducing the phobia or eliminating it altogether. When used effectively, this technique, in his words, "takes the wind out of the sails of the anxiety by reversing one's attitude and replacing a fear with a paradoxical wish."[9] Instead of fighting the fear, the person is encouraged to welcome it, even to exaggerate it. The person deflates the anxiety associated with the situation by no longer resisting it. Thus, "while anxiety creates the symptoms over and over, paradoxical intention strangles them, over and over."[10]

Frankl's writing provides many instances in which he used the technique with his patients. Two examples stand out because they involve a work-related or workplace situation. In one case, the patient was a bookkeeper who was in extreme despair, confessing that he was close to suicide. For some years he had suffered from writer's cramp, which had become so severe that he was in danger of losing his job. Previous treatments had been of no avail, and the patient was now desperate. Frankl recommended to the bookkeeper that he do exactly the opposite of what he usually had done—namely, instead of trying to write as neatly and legibly as possible, to write with the worst possible scrawl. The patient was advised to say to himself, "Now I will show people what a good scribbler I am!" And at the moment that he tried to scribble, he was unable to do so. Instead, his handwriting was actually legible. Within forty-eight hours the bookkeeper had freed himself from his writer's cramp, was again a happy man, and was fully able to work.[11]

Another case involved a young physician who consulted Frankl because of his fear of perspiring. One day the physician had met his boss on the street and, as he extended his hand in greeting, noticed that he was sweating more than usual. This situation was aggravated as the physician's anticipatory anxiety increased with each new encounter. To break this cycle, Frankl advised his patient, if sweating should recur, to resolve deliberately to show people how much he could sweat. A week later the physician returned to report that whenever he met anyone who triggered his anxiety, he said to himself, "I only sweated out a quart before, but now I'm going to pour at least ten quarts!" Frankl wrote that the young physician was able to free himself permanently of the phobia from which he had suffered for four years, and he no longer sweated abnormally when he encountered other people.[12]

In his autobiography Frankl recalled using paradoxical intention to avoid a traffic ticket. He had driven through a yellow light and was pulled over by a police officer. As this officer menacingly approached him, Frankl greeted him with a flood of self-accusations: "You're right, officer. How could I do such a thing? I have no excuse. I am sure I will never do it again, and this will be a lesson for me. This is certainly a crime that deserves punishment." As the story goes, the officer did his best to calm Frankl; he reassured him that he need not worry—that such a thing could happen to anyone and that he was sure Frankl would never do it again. The technique worked, and Frankl saved himself from receiving a ticket![13]

> *Paradoxical intention is the exact opposite of persuasion, since it is not suggested that the patient simply suppress his fears (by the rational conviction that they are groundless) but, rather, that he overcome them by exaggerating them!*[14] (V. Frankl)

Meaning also rests in the appreciation of the moment. When our awareness is focused on the past or on the future, we lose the connection to *now*. We lose the connection to where meaning is *now*. At work, as in our personal lives, we must pay attention to those around us and to the integrity of the process we are going through. The more meaning there is in the process, the more deeply satisfied we will feel, no matter what the outcome. When we work in awareness of the moment, we stay connected to meaning. Our existence, and the existence of all life, is meaning. Meaning is simply waiting to be discovered, whether we work at a construction site, a bakery, a high school, a movie theater, a multinational corporation, a landfill, a restaurant, a home office, or the White House. By not being prisoners of our thoughts, and by not working against ourselves, we find deeper meaning.

Meaning Reflections

Meaning Moment Exercise Think of a challenge you face in your work or personal life. Now think of the worst-case scenario. In essence, you are doing as Viktor Frankl suggested: exaggerating your worst fears. Although you won't actually experience this worst-case scenario, what does this exercise suggest about your situation? What can you learn from this exercise in terms of both process and outcome?

Meaning Questions

- How do you ensure that you don't work against yourself in your work and personal life?
- What worries, fears, or other negative thoughts are holding you back? How might you discard them?
- How might you use the technique of paradoxical intention in your own work and life situations?

Meaning Affirmation

I will increase my awareness of when I am working against myself.

Principle 4. Don't Work Against Yourself

PRINCIPLE 5. Look at Yourself from a Distance

We know that humor is a paramount way of putting distance between something and oneself. One might say as well, that humor helps man rise above his own predicament by allowing him to look at himself in a more detached way.[1] (V. Frankl)

"I can't stand my students," said Janet, an assistant professor at a liberal arts college. She had worked for several years at the same college but every time I (Elaine) got together with her, she seemed more and more frustrated with her students and her job in general. "When I went to college," she told me, "we respected our professors. We didn't wear earphones in class, we didn't text constantly, we didn't check our email on our laptops, and we didn't start conversations with the person sitting beside us. I can't believe how spoiled these kids are. They expect me to spoon-feed them the material and they can't even bother researching anything beyond Wikipedia. They don't like to read more than five pages before they lose concentration. And after all that, they expect an A in the class. I even had a parent of one of my students call me and demand that I reconsider her son's B. Talk about a helicopter parent hovering over their child, unable to let go." Janet would have gone on and on with her litany of complaints, if I hadn't interrupted her.

"Why do you teach?" I asked her. If I asked a big-picture question, I thought Janet might gain some insight into her negative comments. "Well, what else am I going to do? I spent so many years getting my master's and then my doctorate and there aren't many jobs for me except for teaching. I feel trapped, but the pay and the benefits and the hours are good." It was obvious that Janet felt lost, unhappy, and unfulfilled—and her performance evaluations reflected this. But, most of all, it was obvious to me that Janet was in the wrong job. She was an excellent example of someone who was working against herself; her negative attitude resulted in her own poor grade, despite her best intentions or her desire to be a valuable resource for her students and the college. Janet is also an example of someone who is unable to see herself from a distance—that is, to look at herself from a detached and objective point of view, to see where she could shift her attitude and behavior.

There are many situations where seeing ourselves from a distance and using a little humor would be beneficial—and, yes, *meaningful*. In his book *The Doctor and the Soul*, Frankl offers this instructive example. An ad in a London newspaper read: "Unemployed. Brilliant mind offers its services completely free; the survival of the body must be provided for by adequate salary." By quoting this ad, Frankl was not suggesting that unemployment is not a serious matter; on the contrary, he emphasized that being unemployed is a "tragedy because a job is the only source of livelihood for most people." The ad also reflects the fact that not all unemployed people experience inner emptiness or feelings of uselessness because they are unoccupied. Not everyone, the ad suggests, experiences depression or loses their sense of humor.

The fact that a person may not have paid work does not mean that life itself has no meaning for him or her. Our attitude toward any situation, including unemployment and other major life challenges, determines our ability and willingness to respond effectively. The person who placed the ad turned a dire situation into something humorous because he was able to put distance between himself and the issue. He was able to look at himself from a distance, which allowed him to find meaning in his plight and take appropriate action to remedy the situation. Even the wording of the ad reflects his sense of humor and his innate, distinctly human capacity to look at himself in a detached way and rise above his predicament.

Humor and Cheerfulness

While attending a conference in New Orleans about a year before the devastating Hurricane Katrina, we had the opportunity to encounter and experience Winston, a charter bus driver for attendees of major conventions. To his customers, at least initially, Winston was only a bus driver, someone who made sure that they traveled between their hotel and the convention center safely and on time. To Winston, however, his customers represented an important source of meaning. "Welcome to N'Awlins," he said, greeting everyone who boarded his bus. In addition to pointing out what he felt were significant sights along his route, he asked passengers if they had any questions about the city. He was eager to offer his recommendations to enhance visitors' experiences. He told jokes, got people laughing, and even engaged all the passengers in a chant before the final stop: "Don't leave anything on the bus!" In short, Winston turned an ordinary bus ride into an extraordinary experience.

As you might imagine, not every conference attendee appreciated Winston's welcoming gestures, jokes, and counsel. Some preferred silence, especially in the early morning hours. However, because Winston showed a genuine interest in learning about his customers—who they were, where they were from, what they did, why they were in town—he developed an unusual rapport with most of the passengers. His engaging attitude, authenticity, and ability to connect with others added a dimension to the conference experience that was both memorable and meaningful. Winston showed that he truly cared about people, that he found meaning in his encounters with his customers, and that he was firmly committed to exploring his personal labyrinth—his inner bus route—through his work as a bus driver. Because his work had deeper meaning for him, he in turn brought joy and meaning to those with whom he connected. Importantly, Winston was able to see the bus ride from a distance, from another person's perspective. Viewing himself in this detached way allowed him to connect with others as much more than just a bus driver doing his "job." Many of his riders were new to the city, unsure where to go, unsure what lay ahead. Winston empathized with their needs and, using a little humor, made the journey more meaningful for all.

It might seem contradictory or at least a bit odd to write about humor in a book about meaning. But Frankl believed that a sense of humor is a trait that distinguishes us as humans. We all know dogs who smile—but they don't burst out laughing, especially at themselves, when they forget for the umpteenth time where they buried their latest bone! Humor about ourselves represents the essence of self-detachment, especially when the joke is on us. Many comedians build their entire careers on self-detachment: finding humor and meaning by looking at themselves and their life experiences from a distance. Humor and laughter tells us, and others, that we aren't taking ourselves too seriously. This human ability to laugh at ourselves takes the edge off serious work situations, especially those that deserve, and need, a dose of humor. Through humor we not only show others that we don't sweat the small stuff but we also show ourselves that we're no exception to the principle of self-detachment.

Consider the saying, Whoever lifted their head off their deathbed to say, "Gee, I wish I'd gone to the office more often or worked more often"? To our knowledge, no one has—so far, anyway. No matter how meaningful our work is, its meaning comes from our values, the deeper inclinations of our hearts and minds. Our jobs and work are part of our meaning; they represent our intentions to provide for our families, for ourselves, for our community, and for the world. But they are not all of who we are—they are what we do and how we do it. When we look at ourselves from a distance, we see that life is much more than our work, our jobs, our careers. There is much more to living a meaningful life than our work; with self-detachment, we learn this important lesson.

An instructive example of someone who practices the principle of self-detachment is the Dalai Lama, the spiritual and temporal leader of the Tibetan people. He has witnessed the horrific genocide of his beloved people. Millions of Tibetans, including a large number of the spiritual community of Buddhist monks and nuns, have been tortured and murdered. Yet no one laughs louder at himself than the Dalai Lama. He knows the tragedy of his time, yet he also knows happiness, humor, and lightheartedness. In their book *The Art of Happiness at Work*, the Dalai Lama's coauthor, Howard Cutler, makes the following observation about His Holiness:

> At last things fell into place. I finally understood how the Dalai Lama could claim "I do nothing" as his job description. Of course, I knew that with his lighthearted humor, there was a tongue-in-cheek element to this job description. And behind his joking about doing "nothing," I knew of his natural reluctance, which I have observed on many occasions, to engage in unnecessary self-appraisal. This seemed to grow out of his lack of self-involvement, absence of self-absorption, and lack of concern for how others view his work, as long as he had sincere motivation to be of help to others.[2]

Humor is a great gift. It is a great equalizer. It makes a CEO less intimidating and a cab or bus driver more adorable. Often, an adorable CEO can do more for morale than a big raise. A funny cab or bus driver, like Winston, can lighten up a stressful day.

If there's one thing I (Alex) wished I'd learned to do at a young age, it would be to laugh at myself more easily and more often. Growing up, I was a very serious person—uptight, you might even say. In my early experience, having a sense of humor was more likely to get me in trouble—at home, in school, and at work—than it was to help me deal with life's transitions. I didn't learn to fully appreciate my sense of humor until much later in life. Since then, my sense of humor has enabled me to look at things *and* myself from a distance and try to find the humor in a situation, no matter how difficult.

A sense of humor is usually accompanied by cheerfulness. Many cheerful people, it is important to understand, have experienced real tragedy in their lives. When tragedy strikes, it takes us to the depths of grief. Going through grief can bring us full circle, back to cheerfulness. When we know how bad it can be, we find out, as the actor Jack Nicholson would say, how good it can get. Cheerfulness is *not* a "have-a-nice-day" artifice. It's a way of experiencing the present, no matter the weather or the weight of the world. Cheerfulness celebrates the possibility of finding meaning in the situation. It buoys us up, pushes us beyond our individual concerns, and invites us and others around us to find something to be happy about. This doesn't mean that we hide behind cheerfulness or that we ignore serious situations. We simply lighten up and laugh. A moment of humor at the right time can lift us out of our self-imposed misery faster than anything else. When we detach from ourselves *and* from our situation, we don't diminish or deny the circumstances—we go beyond them. We see, feel, and appreciate ourselves as separate from the distress; we accept and rise above. We demonstrate to ourselves and to others that we refuse to be held prisoners of our thoughts!

Self-Detachment

Let's consider some serious topics that have overshadowed corporate America in the past few decades: accounting fraud and the erosion of business ethics. What could possibly be humorous about the corporate crime wave, and how could a lighthearted approach be used to improve the situation in the years ahead?

The satirist Andy Borowitz, a stand-up comedian and author of *Who Moved My Soap? The CEO's Guide to Surviving in Prison*, offers such an approach—one that balances laughter with serious introspection. Speaking at some of the premier business schools in America, Borowitz has shown that satire can be an effective, if offbeat, way to address the subject of CEO and corporate credibility. Getting business ethics into the open and addressing them humorously can be therapeutic for both individual business leaders and their organizations. His brand of humor can be a useful tool for advancing business education, complementing traditional courses in business ethics. After his presentation at the Wharton School (of the University of Pennsylvania), for example, one second-year MBA student said: "There is still a crisis in how people view corporate leaders. To be able to laugh and find some humor will likely help move us forward." An incoming student responded: "It was so refreshing. There was an underlying lesson of 'don't take yourself so seriously.'"[3]

In the world of emergency medical care, these workers have considerable experience with the principle of self-detachment. Their jobs, by definition, are serious, pressure-filled, stressful, and meaningful. They have to detach from themselves and the situation facing them—often involving the life or death of the person in distress—in order to do their work effectively and with meaning. Yet, during the day, these workers often find time to laugh. Humor supports the self-detachment necessary to maintain emotional distance from their patients, so they can observe themselves and their work from a distance to rise above and deal effectively with the stresses of the moment. In the post-9/11 environment, communities nationwide are responsible for emergency planning for everything from fire and car accidents to bombs and terrorism. In one small southwestern county, dozens of people show up at a monthly emergency preparedness meeting. Among those represented are workers from town, county, and state government as well as the police, the fire department, emergency medical services, the National Guard, environmental groups, the Red Cross, ham radio operators, the health department, and representatives from the telephone and power companies. For two hours, these workers discuss the serious emergency possibilities and how best to respond. But there is also humor, as the group laughs—at themselves and one another—which lightens the mood. They bond together with their humor.

In his writing and lectures, Viktor Frankl described a kind of cabaret that was improvised from time to time in the concentration camp. Although it is difficult to imagine, this form of camp entertainment included songs, poems, jokes, and even stand-up comedy (some with underlying satire about the camp) performed by anyone who wanted to. This activity was meaningful in part because it helped the prisoners forget their horrific situation, even if only for a moment. As Frankl reported, "Generally speaking, any pursuit of art in camp was somewhat grotesque. But you might be even more astonished to learn that one could find a sense of humor there as well. *Humor was another of the soul's weapons in the fight for self-preservation.*"[4] In fact, Frankl trained a friend to develop a sense of humor in one of the camps. He suggested to this friend that they promise each other to invent at least one amusing story daily, and it had to be about some incident that could happen after their liberation. One story involved a future dinner engagement, during which Frankl's friend would forget where he was when the soup was served and beg the hostess to ladle it "from the bottom." This request was significant because the camps provided only thin watery soup; servings "from the bottom," which were extremely rare, might include peas and therefore would be a special treat!

It's important to distinguish between *self-detachment* and *denial*. When we *self-detach*, we do so consciously and with an orientation toward action. We understand our predicament and choose to behave in a way that supports our relationship with others. We might share our burden at work; we might not. But we know what it is and we know what we are doing. In contrast, *denial* often means we simply ignore what is happening to us or around us. Denial, in other words, separates us from our experience and the benefits that can be derived from it. When we deny our own experience, we deny the experience of others. Denial thus leads to disconnection. Self-detachment, however, leads to connection, learning, and growth.

Practicing self-detachment also opens up opportunities to learn about others in meaningful ways. Indeed, we never know what's really going on in other people's personal lives. For example, some of our coworkers, or even our friends, may go home to isolation and loneliness; some may go home to a conflict-filled relationship; others may go home to a happy family life. Everyone experiences both the joys and the grief that life offers: we struggle with making ends meet (rent, car payments, healthcare expenses), with teenage or young or no children, with aging parents, and with all the other demands of daily life. Every day, people around the world rise to the occasions in their lives. Some go to work. They bring with them their entire lives, even as they focus on the work at hand. The ancient Greek philosopher Plato advised, "Be kind, for everyone you meet is fighting a hard battle." Unless they share the details, however, we can only assume what kind of battles people are fighting. Just as we face challenges in our own lives and work, we know that others do as well. Just as we would benefit from the support of others, they could benefit from our support. When we reach out to others and share more details of *our* life, we find more meaning in our own life; we are actually helping others find meaning in their life too. We can learn from others, reflecting on how they deal with life in all of its inherent complexity. We can find meaning by looking at our own life from a distance as well as by looking at our life through the lives of others.

Mistakes

Being able to detach from our own mistakes, as well as those of others, is a very useful skill in life and work. Nobody likes to make mistakes, but when we acknowledge our mistakes, and laugh at them, it can be a huge relief for those around us. What are mistakes anyway but lessons from which to learn?[5] Mistakes are a natural part of living. There's a saying that we're only as good as our mistakes, but first we have to acknowledge that we made them.

When someone comes to us at work and says, "I made a mistake," most of us feel empathy. It takes self-detachment to own up to a mistake, to look at yourself and say, "I goofed," then move on with your work and life. We are at the same time the person who doesn't want to make a mistake and the person who made a mistake. When we dwell on our mistakes, we give them far too much credit. When we acknowledge them and laugh them off, we can act as a role model by reassuring those around us that their mistakes, too, are momentary and not who they essentially are. We should all strive to be like the character Calvin in one particular *Calvin and Hobbes* cartoon, in which he trips and falls down, only to get up with arms outstretched to say, "TA-DAAA!!!" We should all say "TA-DAAA" to our mistakes and, more importantly, say "TA-DAAA" to life.

Of course, mistakes come in all shapes and sizes. The large ones might not seem like they are fuel for humor, but they are always life lessons that teach us humility and, deep down, meaning. They teach us that we are more than even our most terrible mistakes.

Developing the Skill of Self-Detachment

Viktor Frankl frequently employed the technique of self-detachment during his imprisonment in the concentration camps. Often he kept himself going by imagining himself as an observer rather than as a prisoner. Here's how he disclosed to one conference audience how he had used self-detachment for his own survival:

> I repeatedly tried to distance myself from the misery that surrounded me by externalizing it. I remember marching one morning from the camp to the work site, hardly able to bear the hunger, the cold, and the pain of my frozen and festering feet, so swollen from hunger edema and squeezed into my shoes. My situation seemed bleak, even hopeless. Then I imagined that I stood at the lectern in a large, beautiful, warm, and bright hall. I was about to give a lecture to an interested audience on "Psychotherapeutic Experiences in a Concentration Camp" (the actual title that he later used at that conference). In the imaginary lecture I reported the things that I am now living through. Believe me, ladies and gentlemen, at that moment I could not dare to hope that some day it would be my good fortune to actually give such a lecture.[6]

Being able to use your imagination effectively to visualize, as did Viktor Frankl, directly supports and illustrates the self-detachment principle in actual practice. Experience has shown that self-detachment can be facilitated by immersing yourself in a role (much like an actor) other than yourself. For example, imagine that you are the principle character in the movie *Defending Your Life*. If you were in Judgment City and were shown video clips of your life's moments of greatest fear (as discussed in chapter 5), what fears would you be confronting and how would you deal with them? How would you justify or defend your past actions? Immersing yourself in such a fictional, yet still autobiographical, detached view of your own life can heighten your sense of responsibility for discovering meaning in your life and work.

Of course, in the final analysis, self-detachment is not about detachment at all. While it has proven to be an effective tool for coping with a wide range of stressful situations, including predicaments and hardships from which escape is impossible, its ultimate value lies in its unlimited potential for bringing wholeness and authentic meaning to life. To summon the power of self-detachment and tap into this potential requires both freedom of thought and a will to meaning. We can only fulfill these requirements if we are not prisoners of our thoughts.

Meaning Reflections

Meaning Moment Exercise Recall a situation in your personal life or work life from which you felt the need to distance yourself before you could find a proper resolution. Perhaps you were faced with a family or business decision that wasn't aligned with your personal values or ethics. Perhaps you were thrust into an emergency situation that required swift action. How did you distance or detach yourself from yourself, so that you could view and review your own attitudes and behaviors? As you think about the situation now, what did you learn from it? In particular, what did you learn about your capacity for self-detachment?

Meaning Questions

• **How do you use humor as a way of putting distance between yourself and a challenge you are facing in your personal life or at work?**

- How could you help your coworkers, friends, or family members learn and practice self-detachment in their lives and at work as a coping mechanism to deal with stress, as a tool for learning and growth, and as a way to find more meaning?
- If you had to watch a video of your life as depicted in the movie *Defending Your Life*, would you be pleased with what you saw?

Meaning Affirmation

I will practice the principle of self-detachment—looking at myself from a distance—in order to gain more insight into my actions and, ultimately, to find more meaning.

PRINCIPLE 6.
Shift Your Focus of Attention

De-reflection can only be attained to the degree to which . . .
awareness is directed toward positive aspects.[1] (V. Frankl)

Sometimes it is the gravity of the hardships or challenges we face that forces us to detect the meaning of life's moments. After waging a courageous, year-and-a-half-long battle with pancreatic cancer, Patrick Swayze, the actor and classically trained dancer whose leading roles in the blockbuster films *Dirty Dancing* and *Ghost* made him a popular movie star, died on September 14, 2009. He was fifty-seven years old. "I'm proud of what I'm doing," Swayze had told the *New York Times* in October the year before his death, when he was still filming *The Beast*, an A&E television series in which he starred as an FBI agent. "How do you nurture a positive attitude when all the statistics say you're a dead man? You go to work."

We all have known people, often people close to us,

who have passed on. We may even have experienced the death of loved ones who have battled terminal illnesses, such as pancreatic cancer or breast cancer. If we are fortunate, we may know people like Patrick Swayze and Elaine's mother (whose story is recounted in chapter 1) who were inspirations and role models in ways that are not always easy to describe. Despite personal hardships and formidable challenges, these people represent human beings at their best, even as conditions are the worst. Observing them, we bear witness to the resilience and unlimited power of the human mind and spirit, and we come to better understand how the search for meaning is the primary intrinsic motivation of all human beings.

Andy is a former executive with a major software company. He used to make more than $130,000 a year and had a terrific benefits package. He supervised teams of software programmers in several states and had an office overseas. But not anymore. Like scores of other well-paid workers, Andy was laid off and has been unable to find a job that offers the same—or even similar—responsibilities, status, salary, and benefits. Instead, out of desperation, he has found himself grasping at survival jobs offering considerably less. "Desperate times call for desperate measures," he says. "This is no time to be picky. Since being laid off, I've sold jewelry in a department store and worked as a cashier at a ski slope, both at eight dollars an hour. Now I sell golf equipment."

Andy, however, is more than a mere survivor in a job market that calls for desperate measures. Although he is empathetic, Andy doesn't really see himself as grasping at straws like some displaced workers. He would say that he's not in the same boat at all. You see, Andy isn't driven by frustration, money worries, shame, or embarrassment. In fact, he doesn't feel that he is going backward; rather, he feels that he's going forward. An avid golfer, Andy has moved on to jobs related to his hobby—first selling golf equipment in a mall sports shop and now helping to run the pro shop at a local golf course. In his current job, Andy sees an even more positive side. "My work is a lot simpler and less challenging than it used to be, but I've learned to be humble," he says. "I see guys coming on to the golf course wound pretty tightly. They're guys who come in and are late for their tee times and they expect me to do something. I enjoy dealing with people who remind me what I *used* to be like."

Andy has learned a great deal since he was cut from his executive job. He has been able to see the silver lining, the hopeful side of what could have been a cloud of despair and a time of inner emptiness. Instead, he shifted his focus to more important matters in life and discovered deeper personal meaning in the process. For instance, he welcomes the opportunity to spend more time with his family, now that he's not flying all over the country and overseas. As Frankl wrote:

> Other things being equal, an unemployed person who maintains his morale will have better chances in the competitive struggle than a person who has become apathetic. He will, for example, be more likely to get a job which both apply for.[2] (V. Frankl)

Throughout my (Alex) own childhood, whenever things went wrong, a voice from inside my head said, "Think about something else." And I would. When I was a teenager, during an equestrian jumping competition, I was thrown into a water jump and the horse fell on top of me. As I lay submerged in the water, I thought about my horse, hoping he was okay and could complete the course. I thought about my horse and his welfare instead of my own. In essence, I was practicing the principle of *de-reflection* by shifting my focus of attention to something else, something more positive than what I was actually experiencing at the time.

Often as children we are naturally resilient; nothing keeps us down for long. Our attention spans are short, our interests many, and our involvement with whatever is happening is complete. As children, most of us knew instinctively how to "think of something else" should someone hurt our feelings, steal our toys, or eat our candy. We might yell and scream for a few moments, but not for long. It wasn't natural to hold onto our thoughts, to become obsessed about wrongdoings. We'd simply get on to the next big adventure. There was always something more exciting to think about and do. However, as adults, this skill often seems to disappear. We learn to think things through, which is useful. But when this type of thinking becomes an obsession and we choose to dwell repeatedly on negative things, it's not as useful anymore.

> De-reflection is intended to counteract . . . compulsive inclination to self-observation.[3] (V. Frankl)

We often wish to have a smooth life, without any conflict. But conflict is part of life. Conflict arises when we think the world should operate according to our expectations or that we should have some control over what others think, say, and do. Conflict arises when we believe our way is the best, or when we think the world isn't fair and we want to restore our vision of what constitutes fairness to the world.

Conflict arises when we feel others are not honoring or treating us well; we might feel like a victim of unjust actions or words. How we respond to conflicts, real or perceived, can trap us in our own mental prison. We spend our time and energy in anger and resistance, becoming stuck, becoming prisoners of our thoughts. Our energy ceases to flow freely, which starts to take a toll on our health—our spirits, our minds, and our bodies.

We can choose to hold onto our anger and resistance, or we can choose to let go. If we let go, we can begin to heal by shifting our focus to something or someone else. We can choose to shift from negative thoughts and negative situations to positive ones. In doing so, we regain control of our emotions and thoughts. This way, importantly, the tension and drama can finally end. When we shift our focus, we often gain new insights into a problem. We can begin to see the situation from someone else's perspective. Remember, there are always more than three sides to every situation. De-reflection encourages us to perceive something new in a situation so that we are able let go of our old attitudes, perceptions, and patterns of behavior. Through this *meaning*-centered process, we are able to mature by transcending those conditions that limit us, so that we can make new commitments. The principle of de-reflection, Frankl would say, helps us to ignore those aspects of our life and work that *should* be ignored.

Focus on the Positive

Years ago, I (Alex) was working in Illinois for the state department of mental health. I was responsible for coordinating social services within a subregion of the city of Chicago, working with an inpatient psychiatric unit in one of the state's mental health facilities. This particular facility, along with others in the metropolitan Chicago area, was overcrowded with patients, many of whom were either psychotic or prone to violence, and my unit was suffering from a severe staff shortage. The facility was so overcrowded that patients were sleeping on the floor in the hallways! I felt that we weren't meeting our ethical and moral obligations to care properly for our fellow human beings. For these and other reasons, both union and nonunion employees complained incessantly about the problems the facility faced. Increasingly, a number of employees avoided work by calling in sick, which made an already poor staffing situation worse. Those of us in supervisory or management positions staffed the agency as well as we could, frequently working multiple eight-hour shifts. Eventually, the complaining and resistance escalated into a full-blown walkout and strike led by union officials.

My boss, Rita, a registered nurse and longtime mental health administrator, said, "Good for them! However, the show has to go on, so let's see what we can do without them." I thought, *Without them? How are we going to do that? We're in a serious predicament with no obvious resolution. Maybe she just doesn't get it.* But Rita knew much more than I gave her credit for. First, she focused on the potentially *positive* implications of the walkout—that we might finally get the resources we had needed for so long. Second, she stressed how much camaraderie was being discovered among those who were left minding the psychiatric unit. We were getting to know each other better, relying on each other more than ever. Rita even invited any patient who had the capacity to help *us* to lend a hand. For Rita, our situation was reminiscent of her medical MASH-type unit in Vietnam. She had survived that situation, and she was sure she would do the same this time around. By shifting our focus of attention to positive experiences, we found the potential for meaning in our predicament. Inspired by Rita's guidance and capacity to de-reflect, as Frankl would say, we were not subdued by our circumstances no matter how dire they appeared at the time.

Creative Distraction

Using our imagination can also help us distract ourselves from certain potentially negative situations, or to de-reflect, as Frankl suggested. Italian film producer and actor Roberto Benigni is well known for using his imagination in ways that allow his audiences to take mental excursions without having to physically travel anywhere. In his internationally acclaimed, Academy Award–winning movie *Life Is Beautiful*, Benigni shared his sentimental tale of a Jewish man, Guido, trying to shield his son from the horrors of the Holocaust. While imprisoned in a camp, Guido creates and plays an imaginative game with his young son, using the game to explain features of the camp that otherwise might have been frightening to his son. By shifting his and his son's focus of attention, from the misery of the camps to a more lighthearted, positive outlook, Guido hides the true horror of the situation from his son and eventually saves him. (The movie has been criticized by those who feel it unrealistically and inappropriately makes light of and pokes fun at events that were so horrific, but Benigni's "comedy" was based on the story of his own father's two-year ordeal in a Nazi labor camp and therefore is grounded in reality.)

Frankl himself also seized on various fantasies to fight off despair during his imprisonment in the concentration camps. He envisioned meeting his mother and visiting with his wife. He imagined himself climbing mountains again—one of his favorite pastimes. He fantasized about personal pleasures, such as having a warm bath, and more public ones, such as lecturing to a packed auditorium. In the latter image, he said, his own ambition helped prevent final despondency. For prisoners, it's often food that stimulates their imaginations and sends them off on mental journeys. They re-create, over and over, the meal they will eat when they are free. In their imaginations they create the colors, textures, tastes, and scents of this food so vividly that the meal sees them through years of isolation and hopelessness. It's the idea of the perfect meal that offers meaning to their lives.

By extension, when we are in a miserable job or personal situation, our choices are to either quit or stay and find meaning in what we are doing. Unless we have an armed guard dictating our every move, we always have the freedom to choose our attitude and, usually, the freedom to choose our next steps. When we are stressed at work, for example, we can always shift our focus of attention to something else: a favorite place, a favorite activity, even a favorite smell. A person we know decorates her office with mementos from trips she has taken around the world. When work grows stressful, she focuses on a favorite vacation spot and, in *Star Trek* fashion, transports herself to it until she relaxes. Another person imagines himself sailing, often using aromatherapy and music to help shift him into the spirit of his vision. Your image of escape could be anything: use whatever works—it's *your* imagination. To quote Albert Einstein, "Imagination is more important than knowledge."

When we become too focused on what's in front of us at work—an oppressive manager, a wayward employee, a complicated task, or a boring routine—we can lose sight of the meaning in our lives. Our ability to detach from any distress and focus imaginatively on something that pleases us can return us to our freedom and to our source of authentic meaning. Creative distraction, or *de-reflection*, to use Frankl's word, is also useful when we have to do something really important at work, such as give a presentation or participate in a crucial meeting. By paying attention to our breathing and to tension in our bodies, and by imagining ourselves in a safe, nurturing place, we can calm ourselves. We can return to ourselves and not be so vulnerable to whatever role we think we are expected to play. When we bring our authentic, centered selves to the situation, even if we don't always know the right thing to say, we speak from our inherent authority, the person we essentially are. This is something to which we are all sensitive. We all recognize when someone is being authentic, and we respond with comfort: we like them and feel at ease. By drawing imaginatively from the source of our authenticity, we can move beyond role playing in our jobs. An ethics of authenticity emerges, and real work can begin.[4]

Exercising our ability to de-reflect difficulties at work, as well as of course in our personal life, helps us to be more resilient. We may even feel more confident because we have a reliable, constructive way of coping when situations become difficult. This mind-set can serve us in minor work-related challenges, such as deciding which project to fund, and in big ones, such as how to deal with losing our jobs. On a personal level, the meaning-centered principle of de-reflection increases our resilience and ability to cope with whatever life challenges may come our way. Our ability to forget ourselves and our problems for a moment and focus our attention on something else can help us feel freer. No longer prisoners of our thoughts, we are restored to an awareness of meaning and thus are more likely to experience life to the fullest.

Meaning Reflections

Meaning Moment Exercise The "Mental Excursion Exercise" will help you practice de-reflection (that is, to shift your focus of attention). It is based on using your imagination to take a mental journey elsewhere in order to gain new, creative insights regarding issues in your work and everyday life. First, write down a challenge you are facing. Now list situations that may be or seem similar to your challenge. Stretch your imagination as much as possible, remembering that you are trying to escape from your actual challenge, so identify situations that are different from each other.

It may help to complete the following sentence: "My problem situation, [*What is it?*], is like [*What is analogous or similar to my situation?*]." For example, "The challenge of having to merge two different organizations is like getting married." Once again, get creative and stretch your thinking! Now list all the steps needed to get married. Some of the steps required in this challenge may lend insight into the steps needed to merge different organizations. Here are some examples: deciding where to live (choosing the best location for the new office) and inviting the families for a rehearsal dinner (inviting members of each organization to dinner to get acquainted before the merger). The "Mental Excursion Exercise" helps you avoid being so obsessed with your challenge that you are unable to see new solutions.

Meaning Questions

- How do you use your imagination to refocus your attention when dealing with problematic situations?
- Think of a situation where you were forced to deal with the fear of change. How would shifting your focus of attention help you deal with this situation?
- How can you help others learn about de-reflection to help them cope with stressful situations in their lives, such as health issues, unemployment, or financial difficulties?

Meaning Affirmation

I will shift my focus of attention in order to gain new perspectives and, by doing so, find deeper meaning.

PRINCIPLE 7.
Extend Beyond Yourself

Don't aim at success—the more you aim at it and make it a target, the more you are going to miss it. For success, like happiness,cannot be pursued; it must ensue and it only does so as the unintended side-effect of one's dedication to a cause greater than oneself or as the by-product of one's surrender to a person other than oneself. Happiness must happen, and the same holds for success: you have to let it happen by not caring about it.[1] (V. Frankl)

Every day Vita delivers our mail—cheerfully. It's her trademark attitude. One day, in miserable weather, we heard her whistling as she went about making her deliveries. Instinctively we shouted out to her, "Thank you for doing such a great job!" She stopped in her tracks and said with surprise. "Thank you! Wow, I'm not accustomed to hearing that. I really appreciate it." We wanted to know more. "How do you stay so positive and upbeat about delivering mail every day?" we asked her. "I don't just deliver mail," she said enthusiastically and with a great deal of pride. "I see myself helping to connect people to other people. I am helping to build the community. Besides, people depend on me and I don't want to let them down."

Vita's attitude about her work reflected the words inscribed on the General Post Office building in New York City: "Neither snow nor rain nor gloom of night stays these couriers from the swift completion of their appointed rounds." The Greek historian Herodotus wrote these words in the fifth century BC. Unfortunately, too often today, postal workers bear the brunt of many complaints about their lack of service ethic and the possibility of their coworkers "going postal." Fair or unfair, the phrase "going postal" has become the symbol of all the negativity a job has to offer: boredom, repetitiveness, exposure to the elements, irritated customers, and a kind of automated behavior that ultimately inspires an explosion of pent-up rage—a killing spree, retaliation against all the suffered injustice of the job. Ultimately, the person doing the job must take responsibility for their choice of attitude and their reaction to the criticisms or complaints leveled at them. In Vita's case, she takes this responsibility seriously. She believes that she is serving a higher purpose, one that extends beyond her own personal needs. In this way she brings meaning to her job, and her work in turn becomes meaningful.

Self-Transcendence

The capacity to extend beyond oneself, according to Frankl, is one of our unique traits as human beings. Indeed, *self-transcendence*, as it is referred to in Frankl's Logotherapy, is the essence of our humanness. Being human basically means focusing on and relating to someone or something *other* than oneself. Recognizing the abstract nature of self-transcendence, Frankl used the human eye as an analogy:

> *In a way, your eyes are self-transcendent as well. Just notice that the capacity of the eye to perceive the surrounding world is ironically dependent on its incapacity to perceive itself, except in a mirror. At the moment my eye perceives something of itself, for instance, a halo with colors around a light, it perceives its own glaucoma. At the moment I see clouding I perceive my own cataract, something of my own eye. But the healthy eye, the normal eye, doesn't see anything of itself. The seeing capacity is impaired to the very extent to which the eye perceives something of itself.*[2] (V. Frankl)

Like the healthy human eye, we also have the potential to experience self-transcendence. This unique aspect of our humanness, however, is a matter of choice. What we learn from Frankl's life and work is that we all have the opportunity to realize this potentiality—we can choose to focus on ourselves and, in some way, be selfish, or we can extend beyond ourselves in service to others. The potential to do either is always within us, but Frankl believed that only in extending *beyond* ourselves will we experience ultimate meaning.

> *In the concentration camps, . . . in this living laboratory and on this testing ground, we watched and witnessed some of our comrades behave like swine while others behaved like saints. Man has both potentials within himself; which one is actualized depends on decisions but not on conditions.*[3] (V. Frankl)

Another illustration of self-transcendence can be found in the humanistic concept advanced in South Africa called Ubuntu.[4] The full expression in Zulu of this concept is *ubun-*

tu ngumuntu ngabantu, translated roughly into English as "a person is only a person through other persons." Ubuntu is not about relationships per se; rather, it is about the way human beings establish their own humanness by recognizing and reaching out to the humanness of others. In effect, by extending beyond ourselves we fulfill or realize more of ourselves. This is because life is reflective. We are more of ourselves because we are connected to others. Living our lives in community gives us a deep sense of humanity, belonging, and meaning.

To gain an appreciation for the reflective basis for self-transcendence, let us share an insightful story called "The Echo":

> *We parked our car snugly at the side of the winding road and began our hike down the steep hillside toward the base of the gorge. Learning not to rush our journey, we stopped to admire the breathtaking view. Before us lay the majestic peak of Crete's highest mountain, Mount Psiloritis, also known as Mount Ida. This mountain holds a very special place in Greek mythology as the place where Zeus was born and raised. As we continued our descent, we remarked to each other how peaceful it was to be in nature. Continuing our conversation, we noticed a slight echo sounding in the valley. "I love you," we each shouted. The mountain repeated back to us, "I love you." We knew at that moment the mountain and Zeus were teaching us something special. Everything we think, say, and do in our lives will come back to us in some manner. Like our meaningful experience in the shadow of Mount Psiloritis, whatever we put out will be reflected back to us in some way—in our own lives, in our own well-being, and in our relationships with others.*[5]

What goes around comes around. Our lives are a reflection of the thoughts, words, and deeds we share with others. Now stop and think for a moment. Are you paying attention and listening to *your* echo? From what life seems to be calling out to you, what are you calling out to life?

Former star tennis player Andrea Jaeger lives self-transcendence. During her years on the tennis circuit, Andrea spent her time off visiting sick children in hospitals around the world. When her career in tennis ended, she decided to dedicate her life to helping terminally ill children have an opportunity to experience and enhance life outside of their hospital rooms. After moving to Aspen, Colorado, Andrea founded the Kids' Stuff Foundation and created the Silver Lining Ranch to host small groups of children with cancer and other life-threatening diseases. "I believe in the philosophy of one child at a time," Jaeger says. "If you can make a child smile or laugh, well, your place in the world has been preserved. You carry a lot of what the kids bring, and when you see the strength, the character, the hope in their eyes and hearts, it gets you through the darkest hours you could ever have fund-raising." Andrea's giving, self-transcendent spirit shone through during an interview with NBC *Dateline.* When asked, "How do you want to be remembered?" Andrea said, "I don't need to be remembered. I want the *kids* to be remembered." In no small way, Andrea's response shows us that the heart's light within the human spirit is most brightly illuminated when we discover meaning beyond our own lives.

The Path of Forgiveness

Often those who have experienced deep suffering rise up to become role models for us, teaching us not to be bitter or stuck in our own suffering but instead to reach out and forgive others. Viktor Frankl, Nelson Mandela, Mahatma Gandhi, the Dalai Lama, Aung San Suu Kyi—all transformed their suffering into service. Meaning, amplified by extending beyond themselves, became their life's work.

Perhaps the most challenging thing we can do to go beyond ourselves is to forgive. Viktor Frankl, as an important case in point, forgave his Nazi guards; he even felt compassion for them. In *Man's Search for Meaning*, he wrote about the SS officer who was the head of the concentration camp from which Frankl was finally liberated. After his liberation, Frankl learned that this man "had secretly spent considerable sums of his own money at the drugstore in the nearby village, purchasing medications for the camp inmates."[6] Frankl, moreover, did not subscribe to the concept of collective guilt whereby *all* Germans, including those of future generations, were to be held responsible for the atrocities committed by their fellow countrymen during the Holocaust. Whenever possible, he fought against the idea of collective guilt, even though it was an unpopular stand immediately after the war.

Nelson Mandela also walked a path of forgiveness during and after his nearly thirty years of imprisonment. Although most of us haven't experienced the same kind of formidable life challenges that Frankl or Mandela faced in their lives, we can learn from them. Indeed, if we pay attention, we will find that life calls out to us every day to go beyond our own interests. We know that, whatever happens to us, we always have the freedom to choose how we respond. We can focus on someone else's guilt, but this only imprisons our souls. Like Frankl and Mandela, we can instead choose to move toward forgiveness.

Forgiveness means letting go of our suffering. It has much more to do with our own well-being than with that of the person(s) we forgive. When we hold on to our suffering—our resentment, hurt, anger—we are inside ourselves with self-pity. Our suffering becomes a veil through which we see ourselves and others, something we have to feed, keep alive, and justify. If we don't, we believe we allow the other person to be "right" in their unjust treatment of us. But forgiveness does not mean forgetting, diminishing, or condoning the misdeed. It has much more to do with freeing ourselves from its hold. We do not have to agree with what happened to us, but we can accept the situation and ultimately let go. In time, we may even move beyond this to have compassion or empathy for the other person or people, having a deep understanding of their behavior and seeing life from their perspective. When we forgive, we liberate ourselves from captivity. As we extend beyond ourselves along the path of forgiveness, we find our own interests are served in ways that are inexplicably and profoundly meaningful.

Miracle on the Hudson

There are many instances where we can be challenged to extend beyond ourselves. On January 15, 2009, US Airways flight 1549 took off from New York City's LaGuardia Airport headed toward Charlotte, North Carolina. Shortly after takeoff, Captain Chelsey Sullenberger ("Sully") radioed air traffic control to report that the plane had been hit by a large flock of birds, resulting in the rare case of both engines being disabled. Although the air traffic controller suggested the plane return to LaGuardia or, alternatively, travel to another airport in New Jersey, Sully realized that both options were not possible and quickly communicated: "We'll be in the Hudson!" Landing the large plane gently in the river was a miracle, but what followed next was a great illustration of Frankl's Logotherapeutic principle of self-transcendence: *extend beyond yourself.*

As the aircraft began to sink into the Hudson River's frigid gray current, witnesses described a scene of level-headed teamwork among passengers and crew to evacuate everyone, including an infant and an elderly woman in a wheelchair. As passengers scrambled for the exits, they did so in as calm a way as possible under the circumstances, so that everyone filed quickly and safely through the exit doors and out onto the wings and the emergency chutes. All of this was accomplished under extremely harsh conditions—most passengers were not properly dressed for being outdoors, and they fled without their life jackets. A few even fell into the 36-degree water, where hypothermia would have quickly taken their lives. Fellow passengers, who effectively were strangers, displayed unselfish acts of courage, risking their lives to fish their fallen comrades out of the water!

Sully and his copilot, Jeffrey Skiles, and their crew exhibited calm and professionalism throughout the ordeal. Sully personally walked up and down the listing, drifting craft twice to ensure that all passengers and crew had evacuated before being the last to leave the plane. Those aboard the responding Coast Guard vessels, tour boats, and commuter ferries worked rapidly to rescue the people from the jetliner, even giving them their gloves, jackets, and coats to prevent hypothermia.

All 155 passengers and crewmembers survived. It truly was "the miracle on the Hudson." What happened on the Hudson River that day illustrates that we can rise above our own individual situation and, against all odds, manifest the human spirit and find deep meaning by extending beyond ourselves.

Team Spirit

Not everyone gets a chance to feel the kind of human spirit manifested on the Hudson. Unfortunately, so many people today feel disconnected and alone, with no one to rely on in case of emergencies or even for their everyday needs. Instead of being meaningfully connected to others in our communities, some are forced to fend for themselves or rely on strangers and institutions for their survival. Some people suggest that this disconnect is a result of technology separating us from each other, but we believe there is a stronger underlying cause. The "me first" way of living, focusing on the individual and individual rights, is what is actually causing much of our loneliness. As a result, our communities are suffering. When we don't emphasize what connects us, we are divided.

We need more "team spirit," whether that team is a group of two or three people or a neighborhood or organization. The term "team spirit" refers to the feelings of camaraderie (and synergy) among the members of the group or team, which enables them to cooperate and work well together. Ideally, we want the results of the team effort to be larger or more significant than if individuals work alone. We all recognize team spirit when we feel it, but what exactly is it? A leading authority on team spirit offered the following observation:

When you ask people . . . what it is like being part of a great team, what is most striking is the meaningfulness of the experience. People talk about being part of something larger than themselves, of being connected, of being generative. It becomes quite clear that, for many, their experiences as part of truly great teams stand out as singular periods of life lived to the fullest. Some spend the rest of their lives looking for ways to recapture that spirit.[7]

Team spirit is bigger than we are—no matter how large our group is—yet it cannot exist without us. Team spirit grows out of doing and being together. When team spirit is alive, anything becomes possible. When we give and take, when we are there for one another, we help raise an individual's spirit as well as the whole team's spirit. When team spirit is high, we relax into enjoying the process of being and doing together. We get caught up in the energy of the team and even the fun we are having together. Creativity flows and productivity increases. Deeper meaning can be found.

Beyond Ourselves

Some individuals live beyond themselves and for others in their work lives and personal lives. Usually, they seem to be doing this because it's in their nature or because they have been blessed with good mentors along their path—including parents, teachers, and bosses, who have guided them by example. Their giving natures may also have grown out of their personal experiences. Perhaps they suffered in their youth, so they want to help other children by becoming foster parents. Perhaps they have a lot of money and have a comfortable life but want to give back, so they joined the Peace Corps. Perhaps they rose to the top of their profession and are searching for deeper meaning, so they connected with a nonprofit organization that serves others. Every day we see people doing things for others—quietly, unexpectedly, and without compensation or the expectation of glory. These are the unsung heroes of our time. If we were to ask these people why they do what they do, they might not have ready answers. But we suspect that they would all agree that it feels good. Selflessness feels good. It satisfies a yearning to transcend ourselves, knowing that we are honoring a deeper meaning in life when we serve the needs of others.

The search for meaning in our lives takes us on paths large and small. When we go beyond ourselves—whether in service, forgiveness, unselfishness, thoughtfulness, generosity, and understanding toward others—we enter into the spiritual realm of meaning. By giving beyond ourselves, we make our own lives richer. This long-understood truth is at the heart of all meaningful spiritual traditions. It's a mystery that can only be experienced. When we do experience this truth, we are in the heart of meaning.

When we work creatively and productively with others, our experience of meaning can be profound. When we work directly for the good of others, meaning deepens in ways that reward us beyond measure. Whenever we go beyond satisfying our own personal needs, we enter the realm of what Frankl called *ultimate meaning*. Other people call it connection to a higher self, to God, to our own spirit, to universal consciousness, to love, to the collective good. Frankl's decision to call his unique approach to psychotherapy *Logotherapy* is significant in a spiritual sense. As we discussed in chapter 2, besides being roughly translated as "the meaning," the root word *logos*, a common Greek word, has deep spiritual meaning and implications. No matter what it's called, ultimate meaning is deep meaning, and when we find it, it transforms our lives.

When we focus solely on ourselves and our own needs, we are being prisoners of our thoughts and our actions. When we spend our lives consumed with our own struggles and our own perspectives, we limit our ability to connect meaningfully with others. Meaning, at its deepest level, is found in self-transcendence—going beyond our own needs and desires to truly care for others. In doing so, we help both ourselves and others. We find meaning in service to others while simultaneously helping ourselves to become more closely aligned with who we truly are.

Meaning Reflections

Meaning Moment Exercise Recall a situation in your personal or work life in which you felt the need to self-transcend, or extend beyond yourself, to deal effectively with it. Perhaps you were faced with a pressing family issue or perplexing customer issue that required an extraordinary response. Maybe you were faced with a question of corporate social responsibility or parental guidance that required some soul-searching for an answer. How did you extend beyond yourself to deal with the situation? What did you do as a result of your shift in consciousness? As you think about the situation now, what did you learn about your capacity for self-transcendence?

- In what ways do you relate to something other than yourself in your personal life?
- Are you stuck in anger about a particular situation or person, or have you moved onto forgiveness or even compassion?
- In what ways do you relate to something other than yourself in your work?

Meaning Affirmation

I will extend beyond myself to find deeper meaning.

MEANING AT THE CORE: Life

*Man's search for meaning is the primary motivation
in his life and not a "secondary rationalization"
of instinctual drives.*[1] (V. Frankl)

The seven core principles we have derived from Viktor
Frankl's System of Logotherapy and Existential Analysis provide insight into how we all can live more meaningful lives.
From our viewpoint, Frankl's work can be summarized into
three key assertions:

1. We always have the freedom to choose. This relates to
   the freedom of will. *Principle 1. Exercise the freedom to
   choose your attitude* helps us understand that, although
   we might not choose what happens *to* us, our *attitude*
   toward what happens to us is always our choice.

2. We are responsible for searching for meaning in our
   lives. The search for meaning is essential to human
   existence. Life has meaning regardless of circumstances. *Principle 2. Realize your will to meaning* suggests that
   we must look for meaning in our lives and we must
   trust that we will find this meaning.

3. We can find meaning in the moment. It's not necessarily about the search for meaning in life per se, but rather the search for meaning in our own lives, in every moment, that matters. Using Frankl's principles—*Principle 3: Detect the meaning of life's moments*; *Principle 4: Don't work against yourself*; *Principle 5: Look at yourself from a distance*; *Principle 6: Shift your focus of attention*; and *Principle 7: Extend beyond yourself*—helps us find deeper meaning in *all* of our life experiences.

We, like so many others, have benefited greatly from the wisdom of Viktor Frankl. In much of our work and personal experiences, we find ourselves referring to his ageless wisdom, especially the seven core principles outlined throughout this book. The key message of this book and from our work in general is that meaning must be at the foundation or *core* of our lives, including our work lives. Without an understanding of the deeper meaning in our lives, we are unable to truly connect with others. Without understanding what brings us meaning, we lack clear direction to guide us through the chaos of life and are vulnerable to and can be easily and possibly negatively affected by outside influences. Without an appreciative attitude, we are less likely to remain engaged and build our personal resilience to cope with all of life's ebbs and flows.

The Crisis of Meaning

As we discussed in chapter 1, there is a crisis of meaning in our world today. Many people have told us that they feel overwhelmed, lonely, and unfulfilled. In chasing the "good life," they have sacrificed their relationships, their health, and their sanity and, at the end of the day, still find themselves with lives and work that bring them little joy and meaning. Depression is on the rise, and many people simply can't cope with the pace of change brought on by technological, cultural, and social transformations. When individuals don't find meaning in their personal and work lives, they are left with a sense of emptiness or inner void, often filled with self-destructive behaviors.

> What threatens contemporary man is the alleged meaninglessness of his life, or, as I call it, the existential vacuum within him. And when does this vacuum open up, when does this so often latent vacuum become manifest? In the state of boredom.[2] (V. Frankl)

More people than ever before, in spite of obvious advances in our way and quality of life, appear to be experiencing this existential angst or are lost in an empty space that Frankl described as an existential vacuum. The term *existential* relates to our existence, addressing such questions as, Why do we exist? and, What is the meaning of it all?

Through our intensive work on meaning with individual clients and organizations, many people have told us they feel empty because they have lost connections with others due to the transitory nature of life—moving across the country; no longer belonging to or feeling connected to neighborhoods, organizations, social groups, religious groups, or political causes; feeling disconnected from society and fearing that their country is on the wrong track; worrying that terrorists will further disrupt their lives and they will have no one to turn to for help and support. People have shared with us that they feel empty because they lack purpose in their day, not having an inspiring reason to get up in the morning. They worry about being left behind in the job market as more organizations lay off workers or cut hours and benefits. They worry about the instability of constantly chasing contract or part-time jobs. Like hamsters on the treadmill of life, they are running faster and faster and still getting nowhere. Older people have told us they wonder if they should have done something more or something different with their lives. Did they settle for something less than they really wanted or expected? People are overwhelmed with financial pressures, drowning under a stack of bills that can't be paid, and stressing about family obligations (caring for young children, wayward teens, and elders suffering from dementia). They worry that their unhealthy lifestyles have led to a vicious cycle of obesity, low energy, and depression.

Many people sense this emptiness, this existential vacuum, but are not sure what to do about it. Some turn to drugs and other forms of avoidance, some put on a happy face to mask the issues, others simply withdraw and postpone living a full life. Although not imprisoned with real barbed wire and steel, many people feel like they are *prisoners* in their own lives. Consider Joshua. From the outside, Joshua appeared to have it all—a successful job, a loving wife, two healthy children, and a few close friends from high school; yet, deep down, he was miserable. He spoke of wanting to drive to the airport, get on a plane, and "run away." He spoke of leaving his wife and family, moving to a new city, changing jobs— signs he wanted to disconnect from his life. Unfortunately for Joshua, and others in a similar situation, running away won't help. His problems would follow him to the next relationship, the next city, the next job. There comes a time when you have to stop and face the existential issues and be willing to change *and* grow. As the saying goes, "You can change without growing, but you can't grow without changing."

The good news is that no one needs to be stuck in an existential void; occasional periods of existential angst notwithstanding, no one needs to be in a permanent crisis of meaning. There are answers. As Frankl said, "Each of us has his own inner concentration camp . . . we must deal with, with forgiveness and patience as full human beings; as we are and what we will become."[3] He was not the first great thinker to make such a claim about the search for meaning being the *primary, intrinsic* motivation of human beings. Thousands of years ago, the ancient Greek philosophers, such as Heraclitus, Socrates, Plato, and Aristotle, talked about the human quest for meaning and living the "good life." Indeed, Plato is famously quoted as having made the following observation about human motivation: "Man, a being in search of meaning."

More and more people are on this search for meaning. An increasing number have revealed to us that they want to feel inspired and they want their lives and work to really matter. They want to maximize their full potential. They want to find deeper meaning, especially in the wake of the country's financial crisis. According to *Parade* magazine's Crisis Impact Poll, "creating a meaningful life" is important to 68 percent of respondents. This does not mean that the other 32 percent are not interested in creating a meaningful life; rather, more than two-thirds of the respondents are now conscious of the need to make creating a meaningful life a priority. In addition, 83 percent of respondents reported that they were reconsidering what they actually need in life. These findings are described as the "upside of coping" with the country's economic crisis.[4] In other words, a positive consequence of the economic crisis is bringing the search for meaning into focus for many people, encouraging them to take meaningful action to cope with the profound changes taking place in their lives.

Meaning Analysis

As quoted in Plato's *Apology*, the classical Greek philosopher Socrates said, "The unexamined life is not worth living." Doing some sort of meaning (that is, existential) analysis is an important part of examining our lives to find deeper meaning. All human beings, Frankl would say, ultimately have both the freedom and the responsibility to position themselves along two key dimensions of life (Figure 2).[5] The horizontal axis in Figure 2 depicts the dimension of *failure* (–) and *success* (+). The vertical axis represents the dimension of *meaning* (+) and *despair* (–), where *meaning* refers to the fulfillment or realization of the person's will to meaning and *despair* is the failure to find meaning or the conviction that life is meaninglessness.

Over the course of their lives, many people experience different degrees of success in their work and personal lives, and they have a shifting awareness of meaning. They thus find themselves at different points on the figure at different times. Consider how people might be placed in one of the four quadrants or along one of the two axes based on their

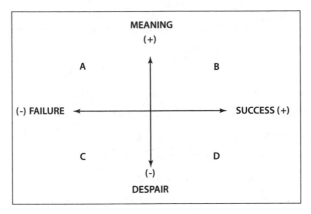

Figure 2. Existential Analysis.

situation. People who might fall into Quadrant D are those who are highly successful in a traditional, material sense, yet unfulfilled, suffering from inner emptiness or despair. An example would be a wealthy business executive who nevertheless may view his or her work as unfulfilling or life as devoid of meaning, or both. In contrast, consider people in Quadrant A in the figure. These people might not be considered extremely financially well-off by societal standards—they may be working in a low-profile job or volunteering for a nonprofit cause and may exist modestly on a meager salary or pension—but they may be quite fulfilled by their work and in their everyday life.

Quadrant B in the figure is the place for people who are *both* successful in a societal sense and fulfilled in a meaning sense. You might recall the story of Tom Chappell (told in chapter 4), cofounder of Tom's of Maine, and how he moved along the vertical axis toward meaning while remaining on the success side of the horizontal dimension. And don't forget the remarkable, inspirational lives of Christopher and Dana Reeve (told in chapter 3). By contrast, Quadrant C is where we would find those people who could be described as down and out. They are unsuccessful in relative terms and, more importantly, unfulfilled, perhaps even empty, in terms of their sense of personal meaning.

Meaning analysis challenges us to step back and reconsider what is important in our lives by asking, What do I want from life? and How do I define success for myself? Some people say they just want financial wealth, but when we dig deeper, we find that most people really want freedom, purpose, good health, and connection with others. In other words, they want to live a meaningful life. When we only measure success in financial and material terms, we limit the value of our humanity. When we only strive for more money and "things," we miss the real journey of life. Meaning is at the heart of what makes us human. When we take the time to know ourselves and honor who we really are, we move deeper into meaning. In a 1953 letter, Frankl wrote, "It is said: where there is a will, there is a way; I add, where there is an aim, there is a will." With less structure in our lives—fewer organizations and groups to belong to and guide us—it is even more important that we know what we want from life (our *aim*) and make the effort (our *will*) to discover what is truly *meaningful* to us.

MEANINGology®

Our work has now expanded to include a broader study of meaning, which we call MEANINGology, defined as "the study and practice of meaning in life, work, and society."

Through our leading-edge research, meaning tests, education programs, and strategic advising, we are well positioned to lead this emerging field of meaning. We call it the meaning movement. Our overall goal is to lead the way to a more meaningful future for all. While the seven principles outlined throughout this book help focus the learning and discussion of Viktor Frankl's teachings in Logotherapy and Existential Analysis, we felt that there was still need for more clarification and guidance on how to put into action the human quest for meaning, both individually and collectively. The specific goal of our work is to take this complex topic, demystify it, and make it more accessible by outlining specific action steps that people can take to find more meaning in their daily lives.

Let's begin with our definition of *meaning*. Many people use the word *meaning* in their everyday conversations but fail to define what they actually mean. Some confuse the concepts of *purpose* and *meaning*, using the terms interchangeably but never actually outlining how they differ. Others say *meaning* is about a "state of mind," "engagement," or "using our strengths." We feel these definitions are limiting and not especially helpful in a practical sense. Still others define *meaning* as "something that is significant" or "something that matters to us." While we agree with these latter two definitions, we wanted to delve deeper, in a Logotherapeutic or existential sense, to consider the metaphysical aspects of the whole study of meaning. We define *meaning* as "resonance with our true nature or core essence." For example, when something feels significant or we know that it matters to us, it is because it resonates with who we truly are—it resonates with our core essence. At the heart of what makes us unique, *core essence* is what defines us as human beings.

Now that we have defined the term *meaning*, how do we actually go about bringing more meaning into our everyday lives? We, like Viktor Frankl, believe that meaning already exists and that it is our job and our personal responsibility to find or discover this meaning in our lives. Through our research and experience, we discovered three common elements or areas for finding deeper meaning that can be viewed as an integration, simplification, and extension of the seven Logotherapeutic principles described in chapters 3 through 9. These three elements form a new paradigm (defined as a unique way of thinking or mental model), which we call our OPA! Formula for Meaning:

- Connect meaningfully with others (O)
- Engage with deeper purpose (P)
- Embrace life with attitude (A)

These three elements spell OPA!—an easy-to-remember, simple acronym, a mantra for living and working that can provide further insights on your path to meaning.

In one of our books on meaning, *The OPA! Way: Finding Joy & Meaning in Everyday Life & Work*, we reveal how we arrived at this formula during our odyssey throughout Greece and via our intensive review of Greek philosophy, mythology, and culture. We outline the three elements of our formula and describe in detail the corresponding nine practices and twenty-seven pathways that have been empirically derived to support these elements. What follows is a brief summary of the three elements of the OPA! Formula for Meaning (others, purpose, and attitude)—all of which, we should emphasize, are closely correlated to the tenets of Logotherapy and Existential Analysis espoused by Viktor Frankl and described in earlier chapters of this book.

Connect Meaningfully with Others (O)

A recent article in *The Guardian* highlighted the issues teens face today in navigating the chaotic world.[6] Although the research revealed that teens (ages 14–21, sometimes referred to as the "Smartphone Generation," "Generation Z," or "Generation K") suffer from the typical teenage angst associated with the pressures of schoolwork and personal appearance, the research also showed that today's teens are more profoundly anxious and distrustful than in previous times. Having lived with their parents' struggle with financial insecurity, 79 percent of the teens interviewed worry about getting a job and 72 percent worry about debt. Only 6 percent of those interviewed say they trust big corporations to do the right thing, and only 10 percent say they trust government to do the right thing—both groups were criticized for not caring about the ordinary person. What was most revealing from the research was that, although technology is essential to this generation, 80 percent of those interviewed prefer to spend time with their friends in person rather than on the phone or online. This generation is far lonelier than many of us had realized; they yearn for connection, especially face-to-face interactions. This supports what Aristotle said many centuries ago: "Man is by nature a social animal." As humans, we are social beings and, at our core, we crave interacting and belonging with others.

Connecting meaningfully with others is the first element in the OPA! Formula for Meaning. We can connect more meaningfully by viewing our interactions with others as being part of a village. Metaphorically speaking, we use the concept of "the village" to define and describe many groups of people: from a few family members to a collection of people in a neighborhood, organization, city, or even nation. What makes a village is not the number of people in the group but the synergistic energy that is shared between and binds the people who choose to belong to the village. The crisis of meaning is partly due to the lack of authentic connection with others. We are not at our best when we isolate ourselves. Survival of the village, both physically and metaphysically, is dependent on the collective strength of all those who are in and part of the village. Whether someone chooses to actively engage with the village, or whether someone chooses to withdraw, all actions contribute, both positively and negatively, to the state of the village. The village, as an integrated whole, is actually greater than the sum of its parts because its vitality depends on the interactions of all those who live or work there.

Meaning is maximized when we trust both ourselves and others. When we don't trust others, when we don't respect them or try to find common ground, we hurt our own chances for finding deeper meaning in our lives. Showing respect for others, even when we might not agree with their strong opinions or points of view, is a path to further meaning in our own lives. When we find out what others are interested in, we can connect more deeply with them while expanding our own awareness of the world. When we encounter conflict, we should stop to understand why the other person acted the way she or he did instead of defensively pointing out their flaws and condemning them for being an idiot. In many instances the person who is so busy pointing out someone else's flaws is often doing so to avoid looking at their own flaws!

The village is built one conversation at a time. To find deeper meaning, we must build the connections in our villages every day. We must reach out to others, begin new conversations, and show that we care about something *beyond* ourselves. By doing so, we demonstrate that we understand that we cannot thrive alone; we are dependent on others. The village gives us a sense of comfort, knowing that someone will be there for us and we, in turn, will be there for them. We will have meaning in our own lives as long as others need us and we need them. We need to ask ourselves if we truly honor others in our villages. Do we strive to form authentic relationships with others, or are we simply passing through, using others to serve our needs? Do we surround ourselves with encouraging people who inspire the possibilities in life, or do we settle for the mediocre, with the majority of our interactions being superficial communications (such as texting or via social media platforms like Facebook)?

In our MEANINGology practice, we have developed three tests designed to gauge a respondent's current level of thinking and feeling regarding the state of meaning in their life and work as well as within a team or organizational setting. The tests provide a score in each of the three elements of our meaning formula: others, purpose, and attitude. Interestingly, the highest scores recorded in our MEANINGology Life test are for the element "others." Many participants report that they are doing well in the area of connecting meaningfully with others, especially when compared to their test scores for the purpose and attitude dimensions (described below). More respondents feel that they find meaning through connecting with others than by other means. This reinforces the fact that building meaningful relationships is an important part of the human quest for meaning.

Engage with Deeper Purpose (P)

Years ago, at a family gathering, we asked our little niece Anna, who was about four at the time, what she was going to be when she grew up. Anna turned to us and answered confidently, "An adult." Her answer was met with a round of laughter around the dinner table. To this day, we think that Anna's innocent response was the most candid of any answers we have heard to that common question. We typically expect people to respond with a chosen field of study or work. Perhaps to receive a more meaningful answer, however, we should instead ask, *Who* do you want *to be* when you grow up?—an inquiry that is not tied to a specific work or career path.

Engaging with deeper purpose is the second element in our OPA! Formula for Meaning. It is important to note that *purpose* and *meaning* are not the same thing. Unlike purpose, meaning is not a destination per se because it doesn't stop when we find it—or at least when we think that we've found it—and it exists, as Viktor Frankl espoused, at all times in life. Purpose is an integral part or element of the overall concept of meaning. Having a purpose—especially one that helps define and guide life—is, of course, an important matter. However, not everyone may be fortunate enough to find or fulfill their purpose in life. Perhaps their lives are cut short by a tragic accident, as a consequence of war or natural disaster, or from an incurable disease. Or perhaps they found some type of purpose in their day but felt that this purpose was weak in connection with whom they felt they truly were. Such misfortunes may leave us wondering about and saddened by lives that did not have the opportunity to fulfill their full potential.

But even though someone's life purpose may not have been fully revealed or fulfilled, it does not mean that their lives did not have meaning. On the contrary, *all* life has meaning. Even if someone's connection to purpose may be weak, a person can still find meaning by connecting meaningfully with others (O) and embracing life with attitude (A), the third element of our OPA! Formula for Meaning (described later in this chapter). What does the expression "living the good life" mean? When we ask people in North America to define it, most conversations revolve around the pursuit of financial and material wealth; but in Greece the focus on accumulating financial wealth is overshadowed by the express need to live a life of purpose. This purpose usually involves knowing oneself, committing to authentic values and goals, and reaching out beyond oneself to be of service to others. In essence, this approach focuses on making a *life*, not making a *living*.

Many people hide who they are in order to fit in with the expectations of others. How often have you witnessed someone trying to be someone they are not? We once attended a dinner party where it was very obvious that the hostess was trying to be someone she was not, acting the role of a sophisticate and a member of high society as depicted in the television show *Downton Abbey*! It was sad to see, for the woman was at her core very lovely but for some reason she felt the need to put on airs. In other cases, people are pressured to follow a path chosen by parents and guardians, even though deep down, that path may have been vicariously chosen for the parents or guardians. In my (Elaine's) situation my father decided early on that I should become a tax accountant (not an expression of my core essence!). When I ultimately chose a job path opposite to his choice, he withdrew support for me in a manipulative way to steer me back onto his preferred track. Fortunately, I realized at a young age that my core essence, my true nature, was not what *my parents* told me it was. I knew intuitively that I was responsible for creating my own life and that I must follow my own path. As the ancient Greek playwright and philosopher Euripides so wisely said: "There is just one life for each of us: our own." Our time on Earth is short; we must not waste it by living someone else's life.

Much of the discussion about purpose tends to revolve around choosing tasks or work in the form of a job or career. However, we feel strongly that we need to look deeper. At the very heart of the meaning challenge is the quest to know oneself and then to use this knowledge to shape a full life of meaning. Purpose, as part of the OPA! Formula for Meaning, is about your search for identity and understanding your core essence. Every living thing in the world has a natural state and qualities or attributes that make it who it is. Our greatest challenge in life is to discover and then embrace our core essence. Being depressed and feeling disconnected are often signs that we are not living in accordance with our core essence and not realizing our highest potential. From an existential perspective, we will only find fulfillment in life when we connect with our core essence.

Many people have asked us, "How do I find my core essence?" Our advice is always personalized, but here are some common recommendations:

- **All experiences can teach you about yourself.** You can never really be off your path since all experiences have meaning, and if you step back and look at them with fresh eyes, you will realize that each experience can provide insight into who you really are. We call these experiences "mini-meanings," clues to help you identify your unique path. Some people suggest that you will know your purpose and your path if you are having fun. We disagree. All experiences, seemingly positive or negative, whether enjoyable or not, provide learning and, as a result, opportunities for personal growth. Life is not about the quest for pleasure; rather, it is about the quest for meaning.

- **Reframe your life in a larger context.** Become more aware of the patterns in your life. Recognize and understand if you are repeating behaviors—such as reacting the same way in certain situations or recycling experiences that may or may not be serving your highest good or best interests. Like a scene from the popular film

Meaning at the Core: Life

Groundhog Day, in which the main character is doomed to relive the same day over and over again until he gets it right, you may be repeating these patterns until you learn a certain lesson. You may have made decisions that resulted in your life evolving in a certain direction that you now realize is not what you really want. You may have to give up some of your current life, including a shift in attitude, in order to become who you authentically want to be. Remember, you can change without growing, but you can't grow without changing!

- **Ask others for their insights.** Be open to new perspectives so that you can broaden your understanding of yourself. Learn about your "shadow side" or "dark side"—the aspects of your personality that you don't know much about or may have repressed because they don't fit the image you are trying to portray or project to others. Learn about your strengths *and* weaknesses. They all provide valuable insights into who you really *are* as you move along your path to finding deeper meaning and realizing your highest potential. In this regard, we have found in our work with clients of all kinds that the SWOT analysis technique (looking at your personal strengths, weaknesses, opportunities, and threats), used by organizations for strategic planning and competitive analysis, is very useful for conducting a personal *meaning* analysis. By faithfully identifying your key attributes and categorizing them according to the SWOT format, ideally by yourself *and* with the help of others, you expand the horizons of truly understanding yourself in a real-world context.

- **Look beyond yourself to find purpose.** Actualizing your full potential involves using your talents, character, and values to help others. Ask yourself *how* you are drawn to help and *what* you are passionate about doing, as a positive and meaningful way of contributing to the world. Put differently, in a quote attributed to the famous Spanish artist Pablo Picasso: "The meaning of life is to find your gift. The purpose of life is to give it away."

- **Reconnect with your childhood.** Understanding your core essence or true nature often involves returning to what you naturally like to do. You can benefit from reviewing what naturally energized you as a child.

Making the effort to reconnect with your core essence will help you build a life of meaning for yourself, instead of being or feeling pressured by outside opinions and comments to live a life that is not yours. To Viktor Frankl, being able to question our lives was a manifestation of being truly human: "No ant, no bee, no animal will ever raise the question of whether or not its existence has a meaning, but man does. It's his privilege that he cares for a meaning to his existence. He is not only searching for such a meaning, but he is even entitled to it. . . . After all, it's a sign of intellectual honesty and sincerity."[7]

Embrace Life with Attitude (A)

Why do some people seem more capable of coping with life's challenges than others? Why do some people choose to see the glass of life as half full while others see it as half empty, or even half empty and leaking? Embracing life with attitude is

Figure 3. The Meaning Difference.

the third element in our OPA! Formula for Meaning. Having a resilient and appreciative attitude involves embracing *all* of life: the ups and the downs, the joys and the sorrows, the good times and the not-so-good times. Without this type of attitude, it is difficult to find meaning (Figure 3).

Meaning is the energy or fuel that motivates us to achieve our full potential as human beings. We must keep track of our meaning "fuel gauge" to determine if we are drained of energy or full of energy. As with our cars, we can't run on empty. We can't constantly feel apathetic, bored, cynical, indifferent, disenchanted, or imprisoned. We must strive to find meaning in our lives and keep the fuel gauge as full as possible so that we have the energy to deal effectively with life's challenges and achieve our highest potential.

Change is inevitable, yet so many people are endlessly striving for "balance" in their life. Such balance is an illusion, however. Heraclitus, the ancient Greek philosopher who was a contemporary of the Buddha and Lao Tzu, is known for his timeless insights about change: "You never step into the same river twice" and "Everything is in flux." The river, like life, is always flowing and changing, and we do not have any control over the river or life. Building personal *resilience*—the ability to recover from or adjust easily to change—is far more valuable and effective at reducing stress and finding meaning in the moment than trying to control life's activities or events.

On our travels we have witnessed firsthand the consequences of trying to control the river of life. Not too long ago, for example, we were in Hong Kong for a series of public speaking engagements. As in other parts of the People's Republic of China, families in Hong Kong often have only one child, and all focus is placed on the success of this one child. As a result, children attend school six days a week, with numerous afterschool programs designed to secure one of the few positions available in top universities in Asia, Europe, and North America. We visited and had the opportunity to speak at one school where the rates of depression and suicide were unusually high, including a recent suicide by one of the favorite teachers. The school was interested in bringing meaning to the center of its mission to deal with such issues as bullying, disengagement, low self-esteem, and other issues facing their at-risk youth. Teaching our OPA! Formula for Meaning was a valuable first step in helping the students, teachers, and administrators cope with the stress they faced.[8]

Despite our desire to control life by only experiencing pleasure and happiness, we must realize that all of life involves struggle. For some reason, we seem to appreciate the struggles depicted in movies and on television, but we don't want to experience those same struggles in our personal lives. Imagine if a movie's story line involved only happy moments—most likely, we would say that it was a very boring movie. Instead, we are attracted, like voyeurs, to films with struggles, drama, villains, and helpers, such as the characters and story-lines depicted in successful films like *The Hunger Games* trilogy, *ET*, *The Godfather*, *The Wizard of Oz*, *Casablanca*, the *Star Wars* franchise, *Titanic*, and the like.

We must embrace *all* of life with attitude. We must understand how our fears may be limiting us and attempt to change how we are living in order to decrease our stress and anxiety. We now know through scientific studies that there are many links between stress and illness. Indeed, chronic stress, such as the kind people experience when facing marital, financial, or work-related problems, affects a person's ability to function and may even lower his or her immunity to disease and illness. How we interpret events in our lives and how we deal with fear and anger can affect the flow of energy throughout the body. How we are able or not able to express our emotions makes a big difference on our physical, emotional, and spiritual health. The practice of medicine is now shifting to holistic or integrated medicine, looking at the context of disease—the causes, not just the symptoms, of disease. Interestingly, this movement is coming full circle back to the foundation of medicine when the ancient Greek physician Hippocrates looked at patients' whole lifestyle to determine the root causes of their disease. We also see a meaningful movement back to the Cretan or Mediterranean diet, eating a plant-based diet, rather than processed foods, which the human body has a difficult time digesting. Shifting the focus from disease and mental illness to well-being and lifestyle can transform our nation's "sick-care" disease-management system into a true health-care system and, in doing so, help people live healthier, more meaningful lives.

When we transition from one phase of life to another, such as graduating from school, moving to a new city, changing jobs or careers, or retiring, many of us face the challenge of adjusting not only our living conditions but also our attitude. It is especially during these times of transition that our perspective on life's meaning is put to the test. Importantly, all transitions in life can be opportunities to grow and find meaning, as opposed to blindly regressing back to the way we've always done things, back to our comfort zones. These are choices that we must make for ourselves, driven in large part by our attitude and by not being prisoners of our thoughts.

Rather than having a so-called midlife crisis, we can begin a search for deeper love, purpose, and meaning that becomes possible in life's second half. Writer Mark Gerzon explores this idea fully in his book *Coming into Our Own: Understanding the Adult Metamorphosis.*[9] Envisioning life as a quest, not a crisis, after midlife is an opportunity that holds great power for all of us. But how we view "midlife" is driven by our choice of attitude. We feel that too much focus has been placed on the financial aspects of retirement and not enough on the existential issues many people face during this particular time in their lives. To retire literally means "to withdraw." Many people retire early but then face an abyss of loneliness and lack of purpose. If they retire at fifty-five, and we've seen many people who do or say they want to do so, what are they going to "do" for the next thirty years (based on average life expectancy)? Chasing their youth with new romantic relationships or erasing wrinkles with plastic surgery will only get these retirees so far on the search for deeper meaning in their life.

Human beings are, by and large, living longer but often

we do not know *how* to live. Midlife and retirement are valuable life stages when we can redesign our lives for fresh and meaningful challenges and opportunities. We are all the authors of our own autobiographies, and we can change the stories of our lives. We can become valuable resources in helping others. After all, life is a creative process, a spiritual adventure that is not dependent on age per se. Our lives are a matter of choice. Live your life with meaning at the core and make your life as meaningful as you can!

Meaning Reflections

Meaning Moment Exercise

Referring to Figure 2, in what quadrant would you place yourself? Where would you *like* to be? Do you have the kind of *aim* (purpose) and the *will* that Viktor Frankl referred to, to move yourself to the desired quadrant?

Meaning Questions

- How do you define "success" in your personal life?
- Describe your core essence or true nature.
- In which area do you believe you are stronger: connecting meaningfully with others (O), engaging with deeper purpose (P), or embracing life with attitude (A)?

Meaning Affirmation

I will strive to live my own life, connected to my core essence.

MEANING AT THE CORE: Work

The struggle for existence is a struggle "for" something;
it is purposeful, and only in so being is it meaning-
ful and able to bring meaning into life.[1] (V. Frankl)

We often separate our work lives from our personal lives but, in reality, they are intertwined. Our work lives take our time and energy and often dictate where we live, where we travel, and how we use our financial resources. Frequently, we bring the conflict we have experienced at work into our personal lives, and vice versa. When we consider the amount of time we spend "at work" (both paid and unpaid, such as volunteering), it should not be surprising that the search for meaning at work is—or at least it *should* be—an important concern. Whether we run a company, drive a bus, cook a meal, clean a hotel room, or help the sick and homeless, our work is a reflection of the presence or absence of meaning in our lives. In many, if not most, of our client engagements, when we ask people to share the most *meaningful* thing that happened in their lives in the last three months, interestingly, more than

90 percent of responses represent experiences from their personal lives, *not* their work lives. Very few participants seem to believe—or at least are not aware—that their work is or can be a source of meaning. Others simply hope that their work will provide meaning, but they don't know how to access this meaning.

We believe that there is a crisis of meaning in the workplace. We've encountered many people who have shared with us that they feel something is missing: they are stressed at work, unsure how they fit with the group's or organization's overall purpose, irritated by their coworkers' lack of empathy and trust, and overall feel disconnected and not fully engaged. The root causes of this lack of meaning are varied. Here are a few insights from our research, interviews, and experience at the Global Meaning Institute:

- Workers often bring the lack of meaning from their personal lives into the workplace. They may not really know what they want in life, so they just put in time at their current jobs, taking the paycheck but not caring about the work, coworkers, or the organization. They may be suffering from exhaustion, dealing with issues in their personal lives (such as divorce, the excessive demands of childcare or caring for elders, or various health issues), leaving them with little energy to devote to and engage with their work.

- Younger workers face their own lack of meaning in the workplace, often exacerbated by the gap between their expectations and the reality they experience. They often suffer difficulties transitioning from school into the workplace and are overwhelmed by the new demands that are placed on them. Younger workers have told us that they thought work would be more fun and a lot easier. Working for eight hours straight is difficult for those who have limited attention spans given their upbringings in high-stimuli, fast-paced environments. They often don't have the patience to see a task through to its end, saying that they are bored, asking for more varied assignments than most organizations can offer, especially for entry-level jobs. Today's youth are attracted to more flexible work arrangements that provide the freedom to complete the work in the way they find most appealing. Some shun the traditional hierarchy found in many organizations. Many young workers don't want to work under stifling "command and control" rules and regulations that they feel result in a loss of individualism. For many young workers, their life experiences (for example, being asked at a young age which movie or restaurant they would like to go to, or simply co-creating a coffee drink at Starbucks) have taught them that they should expect to be equal participants in decision making, but this is not offered in most workplaces. Younger workers have complained to us that they want more access to the leaders and are disappointed when the leaders don't ask for or listen to their ideas. Many younger workers want promotions and feel that they are ready to take on leadership roles, but these roles are proving difficult to attain given that many organizations have eliminated middle management roles and hollowed out their organizations by outsourcing jobs. In addition, many older workers are not leaving their positions or retiring until older, setting up another potential clash between the generations.

- Older workers have complained to us that they resent the lack of respect they sense from younger workers if they are not tech savvy. They say they feel like they don't belong in the youth-oriented workplaces and miss the stability of the "way we used to do it around here." Older workers feel pressured to always be "on," having to constantly check email and perhaps make decisions before they feel ready. They especially resent spending too much time away from their family and friends.

- Many workers, both young and old, feel that the work is meaningless, lacking purpose. Innovation projects, which should be exciting to work on, feel like just another task that needs to be completed. Many workers have told us that there is far too much focus on the financial status of the organization and not enough on the "human side of work." Many are tired of the "games," the conflict, and the bureaucracy.

- There is also a loss of meaning as the relationship between the organization and the worker becomes more tentative. Many organizations, with the objective of lowering overhead costs and gaining more flexibility, are decreasing the number of full-time jobs and shifting the work to part-time or contract jobs, outsourcing jobs, or simply laying off workers and doing more with less. Workers, in response, have less loyalty to one organization, choosing instead to focus on short-term engagements and then move on. It's not surprising that there are lower levels of worker engagement under these scenarios. If an organization is less committed to its workers, then workers will be less committed to the organization.

- Many people we've interviewed have questioned why they should be committed to leaders, when these leaders seemed to be so focused on getting as much as they can get from the organization. There are many cases of leaders earning excessive amounts of money. For example, at Oracle, executive chairman Larry Ellison's compensation package was around $100 million, roughly equal to three thousand times a minimum worker's paycheck.[2] (Of course, many people in the entertainment industry and sports figures also earn excessive amounts of money.) Workers are told that the organization's stock price is skyrocketing, but unfortunately many workers don't own any company stock. They see their leaders drive a Lexus or Tesla into the company parking lot, daily reminders of the inequality. Is it any wonder that some workers end up emulating their leader's behavior, feeling like they deserve more and attempting to take as much as they can?

Disengagement

The evidence of this crisis of meaning is showing up in the low engagement scores commonly found in numerous employee surveys. The Gallup Organization, which has been studying engagement since the 1990s, has reported that only about 30 percent of the nation's workers are fully engaged in their jobs. Alarmingly, these studies have shown us that the number of disengaged employees outnumbers the engaged employees. Based on its research, the Gallup Organization identified three types of employees along a continuum of engagement:

1. Engaged employees work with passion and feel a profound connection to their company. They drive innovation and move the company forward (roughly 30 percent of workers).

2. Disengaged employees are essentially checked out. They are sleepwalking through their workday, putting time—but not energy or passion—into their work (roughly 52 percent of workers).

3. Actively disengaged employees aren't just unhappy at work; they are busy acting out their unhappiness. Every day, these workers undermine what their engaged coworkers accomplish (roughly 18 percent of workers).[3]

According to Gallup, these engagement figures have remained relatively flat over the past five years, despite all of the well-intended engagement investment initiatives that organizations have made.[4]

Other results from Mercer's *What's Working Survey* of thirty thousand workers in seventeen countries echo these alarming disengaged numbers. According to Mercer, nearly one in three workers (32 percent) in the United States were seriously considering leaving the organization; another 21 percent view their employers unfavorably and have low scores on engagement and commitment.[5] In a global study conducted across industries by Steelcase, more than one-third of workers in seventeen of the world's most important economies were found to be disengaged. One of the disturbing questions raised in this study was whether disengaged workers were, in effect, canceling out the efforts being made by engaged workers.[6]

With more than half of the U.S. workforce not engaged (including senior leaders, whose level of disengagement is also high), our workplaces are in trouble. This means that people are not working up to their potential, perhaps showing up for work but exerting little effort, wasting time, slowing projects, and not really caring whether the organization is reaching its goals. Some employees may pass work onto others, sabotage innovation and improvement initiatives, or even steal inventory, supplies, or money. Their negative attitudes can affect the rest of the group, creating a toxic environment for others.[7] They may even not show up for work, claiming fake illnesses or disabilities. These employees stay for the paycheck and the benefits, but their negative or even neutral attitudes affect the whole organization. The level of employee engagement predicts how well an organization performs. Some analysts have concluded that ultimately it adds up to about a 22 percent difference in profitability when top quartile business units (with the most engaged employees) are compared to the bottom quartile (with the least engaged employees). Moreover, Gallup has estimated that the lower productivity of actively disengaged workers costs the U.S. economy about $328 billion.[8] The additional costs of turnover—the loss of knowledge, potential lower customer satisfaction scores, and training efforts for new employees—contribute to the challenges facing organizations with low engagement scores.

The issue of meaningful engagement is not simply a matter of concern for corporations and other business enterprises in the private sector. On the contrary, this issue reaches across all sectors and industries. Leaders in health-care organizations, for example, are increasingly interested in ways to meaningfully engage employees because both disengaged and actively disengaged workers in health-care settings have an especially negative impact on the quality and costs of service—two issues that are central to health-care reform.[9] According to *Forbes*, engagement is still the number-one concern, with 87 percent of companies surveyed considering culture and engagement to be their top priorities.[10] In their attempts to increase engagement, many human resource departments are implementing such benefits as health care and well-being programs, telecommuting, flextime, job sharing, paid paternity and adoption leaves, continuing education, coaching, retirement planning, time off for volunteering, free food, standing desks, and even allowing pets at work. While some of these programs result in increased employee satisfaction scores, many do not. As we see from the Gallup and similar surveys, the level of engagement among U.S. companies has remained stubbornly low. It's time to try a new approach!

Meaning at the Core

The focus on engagement is not the best place to start, however. We need to get to the root cause of the engagement problem and that root cause is the lack of meaning. *The failure to enlist employees in meaning is the root of most engagement issues*. It is a key reason why many innovation initiatives are difficult to sustain and fail in the end. Our research and field experience in innovation management have shown that these initiatives are often not rooted in a meaningful goal, so employees see them as just another task.

There needs to be a deeper understanding of what Viktor Frankl referred to as the "primary, *intrinsic* motivation of human beings"—the search for meaning. Pay raises, incentives, special perks and programs are all *extrinsic*—they come from the outside. We need to start with the intrinsic motivators, those that originate *within* the individual. True engagement begins with personal meaning, understanding ourselves (our interests, talents, and motivations), before we move onto understanding the meaning of actual work, including how we contribute to it and what affect the work has on others within the organization and for society as a whole. If we can connect with the deeper meaning within ourselves *and* the deeper meaning of our work, we will be more engaged. In short, meaning *before* engagement!

Our meaning work at the Global Meaning Institute has demonstrated that starting with and working from the core of meaning is the main driver behind engagement and resilience, health and well-being, and performance and innovation (Figure 4). For example, the outdoor clothing and gear company Patagonia is focused on two things: building the best products possible and causing no harm. The business inspires and implements solutions for the environmental cause. Everyone working with Patagonia understands the deeper meaning of the organization and, through this awareness, can find meaning in their own work. Patagonia's Footprint Chronicles and

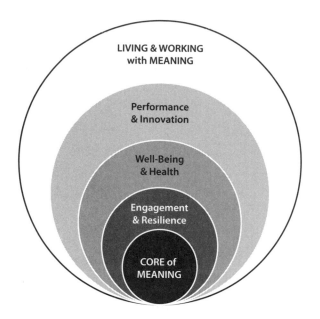

Figure 4. Core of Meaning.®

Common Thread initiative help to further reinforce this understanding and build trust and meaningful engagement among employees. When tough times arise, workers can remind themselves of the greater meaning of their work and thus build resilience.

Understanding *why* we do what we do also improves our ability to manage stress. When we identify the meaning of our work, we increase the energy we have, enhancing our levels of well-being and health. Higher performance and innovation can be achieved through a meaning-centered approach to work. Apple is an example of an organization dedicated to helping others find deeper meaning by exploring and expressing their own creativity. Vancity, one of the largest credit unions in North America, is focused on contributing to its members' and employees' sense of meaning through its community leadership and social well-being initiatives, which are reinforced by the organization's aspirational slogan "Make good money." An increasing number of people are questioning the meaning of their work. They want to know, as with life itself, that their work truly matters and that they are making a difference—to themselves, for others, and even for the larger community or society.

We *can* find the meaning in our work, no matter what the circumstances. We can find meaning cleaning dirty bathrooms or hotel rooms, in rewriting a document over and over again, in bringing food to a restaurant table of rowdy college students, or in flying an airplane full of irate passengers who are upset that the flight is behind schedule. In the workplace we can either choose actively to look for and find meaning, or we can see our jobs as something outside our "real" lives. If we choose the latter, we cheat ourselves out of an enormous amount of life experience. Even if we think we hate our jobs, by stopping long enough to connect what we are doing to our broader relationship to meaning, we can find rewards. The question, of course, is do we want to make such a meaningful connection?

Meaning at work is not a luxury. It can be what inspires us to get through the day. A national *Work/Life Survey* conducted for Philips North America in May 2013 found that American workers were even willing to take a pay cut for more personally meaningful jobs/careers that, among other things, would allow them to create a legacy in life through work and be deeply engaged while doing it.[11] So how do we find the meaning of our work and the meaning in our workplaces? We return to MEANINGology and the OPA! Formula for Meaning to provide a valuable framework and practical tools for understanding and finding deeper meaning at work. Our meaning-centered formula, which was introduced in chapter 10, "Meaning at the Core: Life," involves three core elements: connect meaningfully with others (O), engage with deeper purpose (P), and embrace life with attitude (A). Let's apply the OPA! formula to the challenge of finding meaning at work.

Connect Meaningfully with Others (O)

How we interact with others at work can provide meaning throughout our day. Meaning can be found anywhere. Recall the story of the bus driver, Winston, profiled in chapter 7, who saw each bus-driving moment and each passenger as an opportunity for a meaningful connection. Even though his customers pass fleetingly through his life, Winston found meaning through the *experience* of sharing his day with others. In the thinking of Viktor Frankl, this is an illustration of "realizing experiential values"—an important source of meaning.[12]

Most people we have interviewed through our meaning work, including our clients who represent a broad range of backgrounds and working environments, want to be meaningfully connected to the people with whom they work. Most want to feel a sense of belonging to the collective "village," which is an integral part of the OPA! Formula for Meaning. Many told us they want to belong at work because they didn't feel a sense of community or "village" in other areas of their lives. They want kinder, more humane workplaces where they have the opportunity to connect with, care about, and appreciate others; in turn, they hope others will care about and appreciate them. Some people felt that they were not being honored as equal members of their work community, feeling that they were carrying more than their fair share of the workload and not being recognized or rewarded for their contributions.

As we see in the Core of Meaning figure (above), meaning is the foundation for building the culture of any organization. Everything shapes this *meaning culture*—the words that are used, the stories that are told, the expectations of how work is to be performed, the style of leadership, the "games" people play, the gossip that is allowed to circulate, how promotions and praise are given, how negative behavior is dealt with, how changes in direction are explained, and so on. Meaning takes place in the context of how this community is built each day. Simple things, like referring to the group gathering as "creating a sense of community" instead of the typical "cross-functional offsite," signals to everyone that the goal of the gathering is to bring people together, to build a community with a shared purpose. Every job contributes in some way to the organization. The value of the individual and his or her contribution is recognized. If we treat others like they make a difference, they will. Importantly, this kind of recognition strengthens the ties that bind individual contributors together and fosters a spirit of community that otherwise would not be possible. Building on Viktor Frankl's System of Logotherapy, this interpretation takes us back to its root word, *logos*, which (as we pointed out in chapter 2) has deep spiritual and profound practical implications for understanding the nature of human motivations.

Creating the work village can be more of a challenge when the size of the organization is large and, especially, when the village is mobile or virtual. Authentic connections are harder to form when we don't know the people with whom we are supposed to work and when we don't have face-to-face experiences with them. With organizations shifting to new, flexible design platforms where a core group of people set the goals and coordinate the work, with the rest being contract or freelancers contributing their unique skills, it is more of a challenge to find shared meaning. Such efforts as using online visual communication tools like Skype put a "face to the name." Some organizations are creating a virtual village with online video profiles of group members. These efforts represent small ways to create a more *humanistic* community. As human beings, at our core we are wired for relationships, so anything we can do to show that we care about connecting with others is a step in the right direction.

Top-down innovation, where the senior managers are responsible for identifying all innovation initiatives, might have been a good approach in the past when markets were more stable, but with the volatility and complexity of today's markets, a more inclusive and collaborative approach is needed. Creating a meaning-centered culture involves inviting everyone to offer their innovative insights and ideas to help the organization reach its goals. Besides, most employees want to have more input into shaping the direction and the decisions that are being made. As we know from our twenty-plus years working in innovation management, innovation must happen at all levels of an organization. Creating a meaning-centered culture means creating a safe environment where *all* employees (as well as external partners) feel free to provide input. We also need to address the paradox facing many leaders who ask employees for new ideas and to "think outside the box" but then hold on tightly to old organizational structures and processes that were built solely for efficiency and control.

So who is responsible for creating the meaning-centered culture? It is interesting to note that some of the questions from well-known engagement surveys seem to focus only on what the organization can do *for* the employee, eliciting responses such as "My supervisor seems to care about me as a person," "There is someone at work who encourages my development," and "In the last week, I have received recognition or praise for doing good work." These types of questions reinforce the expectation that the leaders or managers in the organization are solely responsible for creating the culture of meaning. This is the wrong approach. All participants must realize that they are an integral part and are responsible for creating the meaning-centered culture. We need to leave our self-centeredness behind and reach out to appreciate everyone's role in creating the whole village.

Engaging with Deeper Purpose (P)

It all starts with meaning. When I (Elaine) was asked to speak about creating meaningful innovation at Mayo Clinic, I didn't realize that the event would have such a profound effect on . . . me! Mayo Clinic, well known for its advanced medical care, did what I believe is a rare occurrence at many organizational conferences—they brought in two of their "customers," a husband and wife who both were cancer patients being treated at Mayo. The couple spoke candidly about their upset and fear upon hearing their individual diagnoses, their trepidation about having to face numerous medical procedures, and the pain they endured. What was remarkable about their stories was how much respect and love they had for the Mayo staff. At all stages of the experience, the staff seemed to have created a healing environment not just for these two but also for their Mayo coworkers. They seemed to know that working at Mayo was an opportunity to share meaning with all people, not just the patients. From the admissions department to in-patient treatment to aftercare, meaning was found at all stages of the process. After the husband and wife finished speaking, there wasn't a dry eye in the room, mine included.

Perhaps it may seem easier to see the direct line to meaning in a health-care setting. But this need not be the case if an employee understands the overall purpose of the work and can see the meaning in what they do individually. For example, a worker at an online fulfillment center, such as Amazon, might connect to the meaning behind packing a birthday present for a child, packing a book for enlightenment and learning, or simply saving people money so they can live better. A receptionist might find meaning in directing people to the right office, in lessening the stress of office visitors, or in coordinating the flow of paperwork to help others. A funeral director might connect to the meaning of helping people deal with the shock of death. Even in what could be considered the mundane job of flipping burgers, meaning could be found in serving food to people on the run or in helping people on a budget still experience the joy of eating out.

What matters most is that an employee find the link between the overall purpose of the organization and how that purpose helps them discover meaning for themselves. Unfortunately, many organizations do not know what their purpose is, other than making money. They lose track of the reason the organization exists. When a clear purpose is missing, or if the leaders of an organization fail to communicate and develop a common understanding of what the purpose is to all employees, employees don't know what is expected of them and they have to check in all the time to see if they are making the right decisions. If employees don't know how their work is connected to and contributes to the bigger picture, they can't see themselves as an essential part of the organization. They won't feel that they matter or that the work that they do matters. Leaders should not take for granted that people will see this connection or that people understand what the organization needs them to do and why.

For us, an organization's purpose (the reason for doing something) and its mission (an important assignment) are closely related. We call this overlap the *meaning mission*. All organizations need to clarify their meaning missions, which drive the entire organization. Some organizations have strong meaning missions: Starbucks's mission is to inspire and nurture the human spirit, one person, one cup, one neighborhood at a time. Hallmark's meaning mission is to celebrate life's little moments, Southwest Airlines's mission is to democratize air travel, Trader Joe's mission is to bring joy and enthusiasm to the customer experience, and Johnson &

Johnson's mission is to alleviate pain and suffering. We have defined meaning as the resonance with our core essence or true nature. These meaning mission statements help clarify the core essence or true nature of these organizations. Most important, the meaning mission must be authentic. We once worked with an organization whose mission was stated as "helping people eat healthier," but we were dismayed when the company proudly revealed its new product of the year—a type of processed, sugary, high-calorie dessert!

Many organizations are undergoing major transformations that are humanizing the workforce and focusing on the deeper meaning of the work itself. As technology takes over the routine aspects of an organization, the need for a stronger focus on meaning and also on stronger leadership skills grows. Every organization is a dynamic, social process—not a static organizational chart or structure. Great leaders understand the human side of work and, most important, why meaning must be the foundation for the enterprise. As Donald Berwick, MD, a health-care improvement expert and former administrator in charge of the Medicare and Medicaid programs in the United States, so wisely said: "The leader who thinks that it is enough to create report cards and contingent rewards misses the biggest and hardest opportunity of leadership itself—to help people discover and celebrate the meaning in their work. . . . We know that the magic is in the meaning."[13]

As Viktor Frankl taught, the will to meaning is the most fundamental of human motivations. We believe further that the fundamental role of leadership is to help people find and connect to the deeper meaning of their work. A leader does so first by tapping into the deeper meaning of their *own* work and, then, by creating the conditions that enable others to search for meaning in *their* work. In other words, leaders must lead *with* and *to* meaning. In essence, the leader's number-one job is to champion meaning in the organization, which will drive engagement and resilience, health and well-being, and performance and innovation to higher levels. Against this backdrop, we call for organizations to replace the typical management hierarchy and conventional leadership paradigm with this philosophy of "meaning-centric leadership." Meaning, in this regard, should be in every leader's job description, and an integral part of everyone's performance review, to ensure that it remains central to the organization's identity and meaning mission.[14]

Leaders can activate people to feel more fully alive and unlock their talents first by understanding how each employee finds meaning. The next step is to help their employees strengthen this meaning by seeing how their work is congruent with their personal goals. By doing so, a leader can help others see their work in a larger context than just the tasks that need to be done. One size does not fit all, however. It is important to know what inspires each employee, their goals, and their styles; some want to work alone on routine projects and simply to get better, others enjoy their coworkers but perhaps enjoy less the actual work, others still might want to take on more responsibility and become leaders themselves. A strong leader helps everyone identify their own individual paths to meaning.

A fundamental part of engaging with deeper purpose is to know thyself. It takes time and effort to question, reflect, and know authentically who we are—not what others want us to be. It takes time to discover what really matters to us, what excites us, what is meaningful. More and more people are raising their expectations of how work should align with their personal values, interests, and talents. They want meaningful work that engages their talents in something they believe in, using their uniqueness and creativity to help others. Too often, people are focused on the question, What job/career should I have? This is not the right question. The question should be, What is my core essence or true nature? Once we know this, we can build our life and work around this knowledge and unleash our full potential.

Embrace Life with Attitude (A)

The meaning of our work is not limited to the tasks we do, the products we produce, the services we deliver, or the buildings in which we collaborate. Rather, the meaning of our work involves what essentially are metaphysical aspects—that is, the "energy" created when two or more people come together and interact. In this regard, meaning at work must consider the *spirit*, not just the mind and body, of each person involved in the interaction. All of these human dimensions are inter-related, and each contributes in significant and practical ways to the meaning or lack of meaning that we sense.

Öystein Skalleberg, the founder of Skaltek, a major equipment manufacturer based in Stockholm, Sweden, pro-vides a great example of an organization that honors the human spirit at work. Skalleberg's formula for building a company culture involves the saying: "*Confidence* is the start of it, *joy* is a part of it, *love* is the heart of it." The company doesn't use job titles, avoiding conferring privileged status on certain people. Each employee's business card carries only pertinent contact information along with a photo. Once, when Skalleberg was asked about this policy on job titles, he responded that if he *were* to give his employees a job title, it would be something like "Leonardo da Vinci or Unlimited Possibilities" rather than the job titles used by most companies. He believes that "every human being is a Leonardo da Vinci. The only problem is that he doesn't know it. His parents didn't know it, and they didn't treat him like a Leonardo. Therefore he didn't become like a Leonardo. That's my basic theory."[15] In addition, all workers who help build a machine add their individual signature to the final product. In this way there is a direct line from everyone involved in product development to the customer as well as an emphasis on total quality management that is completely transparent. An even more radical practice at Skaltek is an annual employee appraisal process that involves the use of randomly selected performance review teams. According to Skalleberg, since no one knows who will be conducting their performance review each year, "Everybody smiles in all directions!"

The late Anita Roddick, founder of the cosmetics and skin care company The Body Shop, argued that all people really want is to be alive in the workplace.[16] Work often gives us a chance to express our opinions and our unique creativity. When it does, it gives us energy. When it doesn't or when we worry excessively, we lose energy. All of us need to better understand what gives us energy and what depletes our energy. In addition, we should try to do things that, as Roddick suggested, make us feel "alive" at work.

The results of a recent global review of Employee Assistance Programs (EAPs) by Workplace Options, described as the world's largest integrated employee support services and work-life provider, showed an unfortunate increase of nearly 50 percent in total depression, stress, and anxiety cases over three years (2012–2014).[17] Many people report feeling stressed often and very often. Research has shown that chronic stress at work can lead to physical illness or exacerbate already existing health-related conditions. This kind of unhealthy relationship between stress and work doesn't stop at the office or workplace. Indeed, the spillover effects can be toxic in one's home and personal life. Employee mental health, of course, is an issue that impacts the ultimate success of every organization. Such a dramatic increase in the number of employees reporting serious mental and emotional health concerns underscores the need to make well-being, and specifically meaning, a top organizational priority.

The loss of energy in spirit, mind, and body is often rooted in fear, rigidity, and a tendency to see scarcity in life, rather than abundance or the bright side of life. By embracing a broader perspective and being more flexible, by focusing on what we want and have instead of what we don't want and don't have, we can improve our resilience and bounce back from setbacks or challenges more quickly and effectively. As Viktor Frankl taught us, we all have the ultimate freedom to choose our attitude and create a different experience for ourselves. In one of our client engagements, we recall speaking with a senior business executive who, although he had an incredibly successful career, was never satisfied with his accomplishments because he hadn't reached the level of CEO (chief executive officer). No matter how much success he had, this executive always focused on the gap. We recommended that he reflect seriously on the lesson and the deeper meaning that this work situation might be trying to teach him. Perhaps not reaching the pinnacle he envisioned for himself allowed him to experience other more important things in life. Perhaps by letting go of his obsession on the gap, which could be a sign of *paradoxical intention* in which he was actually working against himself (see Principle 4 in chapter 6), he might make room for new adventures to enter his life. Above all, we told him that if he would let go, he might see that he was not a victim (or prisoner) of his circumstances after all; at the very least, he always had the freedom to choose his attitude toward any given situation even if he could not change it.

Our capacity to embrace *all* of life with attitude is a key component of our OPA! formula for discovering meaning in life and work. Besides being our ultimate freedom, as Frankl famously espoused, it is the fuel, as well as the starting point, for helping us deal with life's challenges, from the most trivial to the most formidable. Our choice of attitude is the foundation of our resilience and our outlook on life itself. By viewing life with an appreciative attitude, we build our enthusiasm (a word that literally means "manifesting the spirit within") and prepare ourselves to respond to life's call with a sense of confidence and deep meaning that doesn't exist otherwise.

The search for meaning is a megatrend whose time has come. In the world of work, meaning is slowly but surely moving to center stage. The idea of meaning in organizations is gaining acceptance among academics and is finally being viewed as a subject for serious investigation and practice.[18]

Meaning at the Core: Work

As we struggle to reinvent how we run our organizations, the focus on meaning as an organization-wide initiative and key growth strategy is intensifying. It is therefore not at all surprising that the Academy of Management chose "Making Organizations Meaningful" as its annual conference theme for 2016! It is people who give life to their work and to their organizations. Making the effort to find deeper meaning at work and in the workplace can provide insights into our core essence or true nature. It can also spark and sustain the energy needed to work toward achieving collective goals. When we connect meaningfully with others, engage with deeper purpose, and embrace life with attitude—when all three of these elements are working in harmony—we have meaning.

Meaning Reflections

Meaning Moment Exercise — It is important that everyone working in a group or organization understand its *meaning mission*. If one has already been articulated, it would be beneficial to share stories of events or actions that support this meaning mission. If the group has yet to create its meaning mission, a simple exercise to do so involves everyone writing down the three things they believe the group or organization is known for today and the three things they want the group or organization to be known for in the future. Share the insights and look for overlap. Through this process you will discover the core essence of the organization, which can form the basis of its meaning mission.

- What opportunities do you have on a daily basis to connect meaningfully with others?
- Can you describe your core essence or true nature? How would your work be different if you worked in alignment with your core essence?
- What energizes you at work? What depletes your energy? How could you feel more alive at work?

Meaning Affirmation

I will strive to connect to my core essence in order to work with meaning.

MEANING AT THE CORE: Society

We must never be content with what has already been achieved. Life never ceases to put new questions to us, never permits us to come to rest. . . . The man who stands still is passed by; the man who is smugly contented loses himself. Neither in creating or experiencing may we rest content with achievement; every day, ever hour makes new deeds necessary and new experiences possible.[1] (V. Frankl)

In addition to the crisis of meaning in our personal lives and workplaces, there is also a crisis of meaning in our society. The symptoms of this existential crisis echo what Viktor Frankl referred to many decades ago as the "mass neurotic triad" (addiction, aggression, and depression)—a notion we introduced in chapter 4. Unfortunately, these symptoms have not waned over the years; if anything, they have intensified and now manifest themselves in ways that Frankl could not have imagined when he first wrote about them. These societal conditions are symptoms, not root causes, of the lack of meaning. This crisis of meaning in society received attention in an article in the *Utne Reader Online*, where life in the postmodern world is described as displaying certain characteristics and influences that look very much like manifestations of Frankl's existential vacuum:

> *Why am I sad? Why am I anxious? Why can't I love? The answer, perhaps, lies deep in our collective subconscious. The route to the surface passes through the postmodern hall of mirrors. The trip looks forbidding. And yet it is a worthwhile excursion. Think of it as trying to solve the tantalizing psychothriller of your own life, the ultimate existential whodunit. . . . Like it or not, we humans are stuck in a permanent crisis of meaning, a dark room from which we can never escape. Postmodernism pulls the philosophical carpet out from under us and leaves us in an existential void.*[2]

But, of course, Viktor Frankl, who was one of the world's most profound and true optimists, would disagree vehemently with the idea that we were stuck *permanently* in a crisis of meaning. As long as we are not prisoners of our thoughts, we will come to realize that the keys to escaping the "dark room" and to finding true freedom are *within* us, and within reach. This chapter explores what we consider to be the many root causes of this meaning crisis in society and offer a practical way to finding meaning using our MEANINGology paradigm and OPA! formula.

Connect Meaningfully with Others (O)

When we fail to connect meaningfully with others, we are simply individuals living in the same place. We may not recognize that we have much in common, and our interactions may be more akin to ships passing each other in the night than authentic relationships built on trust, awareness of interdependency, and mutuality of interests and benefits.

Against this backdrop, the foundation upon which we build our communities and our society can be destroyed. Here are a few of the factors contributing to the breakdown of our communities (our "villages"):

- We are a more transient population than we used to be. We now more typically move from city to city, country to country, fracturing ties to one specific place and group of people.

- Many people live alone or apart in apartments, often not knowing who is living above, below, or beside us. We may only see our neighbors on an elevator. We engage in superficial conversation or simply look away, missing the opportunity to connect.

- The traditional family structure has been challenged with the rising incidence of divorce or because we are working two jobs, overlapping at odd hours, not eating meals together. Opportunities to connect with one another are limited.

- As the economy moves to more "gig" part-time or contract jobs, we find it is more difficult to form lasting friendships from work. We frequently change jobs, which results in the loss of potential connections from our workplaces.

- On the whole, we are less interested than we used to be in joining religious or social groups.

- We prefer to bury our heads in technology, even streaming movies at home instead of going out to a theater where we might interact with others.

- We are less interested in community affairs and community leaders than in previous decades, as evidenced by our historically low voter-turnout numbers.

- Significantly, we now turn to online news sources that reinforce a particular worldview. As we filter out what does not resonate with us, sooner or later, we fail to see or hear any alternative views. Eventually we find it difficult to interact meaningfully with those who hold differing views. As we view the world through a smaller lens, we lessen our ability to learn from diverse perspectives. Our societies become more fragmented as a result of this increasing myopia.

- We appear to care less about what happens in our neighborhoods, as illustrated by the "broken windows theory." If a broken window is left not repaired, people will conclude that no one cares and soon more windows are broken, spreading urban decay throughout the community.

- Perhaps most significantly, money has moved to the center of our society—everything seems to revolve around money. We often focus on our financial needs instead of on our broader social needs or the needs of the greater community.

These factors have resulted in the loss of connection to our communities or "villages." Many of us feel we don't belong or that we are not an important part of the community. When society becomes more and more fragmented, we lack a common identity and a common sense of purpose. We shift, instead, to taking care of ourselves, focusing more on our individual needs and less on the greater good. U.S. president John F. Kennedy once said, "Ask not what your country can do for you; ask what you can do for your country." Unfortunately, it seems that today the pendulum has swung all the way over to the other side, to "What can you—individually and collectively—do for *me*?" Even though we hear statements like "we live in a global village" or "it takes a village to raise a child," we don't live and act like true villagers! Sadly, we are losing the "soul" of our communities, ignoring the danger that when a community (or society) loses its soul, it loses itself.

The solution is to put meaning at the center of our society, to put meaning at the core. When we focus on meaning, we can create a greater sense of community by rebuilding our connections with and helping our neighbors, by getting more involved in our local economies, politics, and social groups. We can find more commonalities while respecting differences. We can swing the pendulum back from excessive individualism toward more of a concern for the collective and societal good.

Here is a small, but very meaningful, example from Greece. Despite facing a financial crisis, the people of Greece have demonstrated their shared humanity by helping each other as well as by extending hospitality to the flood of refugees who have landed on their shores and in their cities. Two illustrations of creating and practicing the "village" concept are the On Hold and Walls of Kindness programs. In coffee shops and grocery stores Greek citizens are paying it forward by purchasing additional items and placing them "on hold" for a person or family in need. The initiative is now spreading to drugstores, small clinics, and even to hair salons. The other grassroots humanitarian project engages Greek volunteers who hang hooks throughout the community or neighborhood for use by people who are encouraged to hang bags of food and clean clothes for the needy.[3] These extraordinary volunteer efforts have not gone unnoticed. Oscar-winning British actress and political activist Vanessa Redgrave, for instance, who visited debt-ridden Greece in the face of the refugee crisis in 2016, made the following insightful observation about how the Greeks were connecting meaningfully with others: "The Greek people are showing the world how to be human . . . how to try to help fellow human beings."[4]

There is hope. We are starting to see more and more awareness of the need to connect in all aspects of society. We know there is a tremendous need for more shared senior housing so that elders have a chance to develop more friendships or simply have someone to talk with during their days. We know that efforts to build community among younger folks are also taking root. For instance, Smith in Beltline, a new condominium project in Calgary, Canada, is attracting people who want an increased sense of community by offering such unique features as shared spaces for work and socializing, an inventory of bikes for residents to use, and a shared tool library.[5] The "sharing economy" is helping people save money and also helping to build new connections between people, with such services as shared accommodation (Airbnb), shared rides (Uber and Lyft), shared cars (Zipcars and Car2Go), and shared work spaces (WeWork). Community garden plots and the return to farmers markets are examples of this growing interest in (re)connecting meaningfully with others.

We often tell ourselves that we are separate, but in reality we are part of and dependent on the whole. Self and society are inseparable. We need a stronger sense of belonging in our communities to help us find the meaning that we are all searching for.

Engage with Deeper Purpose (P)

We are facing an existential crisis in many facets of our society, including business, government, and education. The purposes and practices of these entities are being closely scrutinized, with many people calling for radical changes to address inequality, greed, and corruption. These calls for change are really calls for meaning. Corporations have been especially under attack for their obsession with profits. It's been forty-five years since Milton Friedman famously wrote that the responsibility of business is to increase its profits. Many companies follow this mantra, ruthlessly cutting expenses, including jobs, in an effort to maximize profits and, with it, to maximize shareholder or investor returns. When the only stated goal of an organization is to make money, however, people tend to follow the money. The deeper purpose and meaning of the organization are lost.

Not all companies are only focused on profits, though. When fire destroyed the Malden Mills factory in Massachusetts, three thousand people were instantly out of jobs. As he watched his factory burn, Aaron Feuerstein, president and CEO of the company, decided that it was not the end of Malden Mills. The first thing he did was keep all three thousand workers on the payroll, with full benefits for three months. There was nowhere for them to work, but Feuerstein knew that it was unconscionable to put three thousand people out on the streets. The company was directly or indirectly involved on every level in the local community. It cost millions of dollars to keep all the workers on the payroll, forcing the company into bankruptcy. But Feuerstein prevailed. He set up temporary plants in old warehouses so the company could start supplying its fabrics to its customers. He risked everything—his money, his reputation, his business. He believed in his employees, however, and they believed in him, working extra hard to get the company back on its feet. The company eventually came out of bankruptcy, illustrating that it's not all about the money. Loyalty and meaning created the comeback, for the company, the employees, and the community.

Consistent with other studies, a survey conducted by Korn Ferry of more than 7,500 business and human resource leaders in 107 countries found that, across all leadership levels, there is a critical need to improve employee engagement. Importantly, the vast majority (87 percent) of respondents reported that linking an organization's social responsibility efforts to leadership development has a positive impact on both engagement and performance. "In today's world employees are looking for organizations that are giving back to the community. Where there's purpose, there's a sense of meaning. There's a sense of value. Opportunities to give back and serve are perfect places to develop leadership." The Korn Ferry study results underscore the fact that people want to work for a company whose culture is aligned with their values—a criterion that is especially true for younger workers. In fact, the number-one reason millennials choose one job over another, Korn Ferry noted, is visibility and buy-in to the mission/vision of an organization. Progressive companies recognize that it isn't good enough to just make a profit anymore; they are going beyond volunteerism, linking profitability with social responsibility and embedding these goals in their core mission statements. "Done for the right reasons, a focus on purpose and social responsibility has a lasting impact on each and every person who comes in contact with your organization."[6]

There needs to be a shift to a more human-centered, meaning-focused approach to business. We call this *anthrocapitalism*—combining the Greek word *anthropos* (humanity) and the English word *capitalism*. Anthrocapitalism is not specifically about corporate social responsibility per se, which is often a separate initiative layered onto the organization. It's not about making a profit and then donating some portion to charity. Rather, it's about a entirely new operating model that starts with putting *meaning* at the core. It's about how the organization makes its money. It's about clarifying the deeper role the organization can play in making the world a better place. It's about balancing economic value with the broader social value an organization can offer to co-create and transform society. In essence, anthrocapitalism is about changing the purpose of business from maximizing shareholder value to maximizing its meaning contribution to the world. The broader concept of meaning, not just profit, is the new bottom line.

We need to put meaning at the core of business. By taking a broader view of the contributions an organization can make to society, we can create new operating models and "next practices," not just best practices, which take all stakeholders into account. We can change our perspectives and worldview from finding meaning in "working for x company" to finding meaning by "working for x company serving this community in this world." We are starting to see more examples of anthrocapitalism in action with such organizations as Timberland, Tom's Shoes, Nature's Way, and Seventh Generation leading the way. Innocent Juice in the United Kingdom ("trying to do the right thing"), Texas A&M University ("developing leaders of character dedicated to serving the greater good"), and Aveda ("to care for the world we live in") are other examples that give us hope! As Thomas Moore, best-selling author of *Care of the Soul*, has astutely observed, there is deep *meaning* in the ultimate purpose of conducting "business" in society and of caring for our "economic" well-being:

> *Economics is the law of life, and in fact this word also has deep meaning, coming from oikos, Greek for home or temple . . . and nomos, meaning management, custom and law. . . . Business involves all aspects of managing our home, whether the family house or the planet, and therefore has to do with survival, fulfillment, community, and meaning.*[7]

We also need to put meaning at the core of government. If government is really about directing and managing the public's business, then there should be ample opportunity for leaders in government, at all levels and in all categories (elected, appointed, and civil service), to shift the conversation from prosperity, in terms of our financial situations, to the broader topic of meaning. As with the business sector, government action that is authentically committed to meaning will drive engagement and resilience, health and well-being, and performance and innovation. This will help to ensure that the delivery of public goods and services by and through government will always reflect a passion for excellence, a concern for guarding the public's trust, and a focus on advancing the public welfare.

As an instrument of society, government's purpose, as the ancient Greek philosopher Aristotle wisely advised, "is not merely to provide a living but to make a life that is good."[8] Doing the public's work is a noble calling and, as such, should be viewed with respect rather than with suspicion, ambivalence, and disrespect. To quote Aristotle: "Government is more than a legal structure, more than an arrangement of offices; it is a manner of life, a moral spirit."[9] For public servants, Aristotle's wisdom strikes at the heart and soul of who they are and what they have chosen to do. It suggests that working in government really does mean something—above and beyond the obvious fact of gainful employment.

At the basic level, society is about how the community bonds together not only to survive but to thrive—that is, to grow stronger as individuals and as a group. Unfortunately, capitalism has often made money the focus of government and the political discourse instead of allowing government and politics to focus on the end goal of building a strong social system that both provides a living *and* makes a life that is good for all within it. It is getting harder and harder to engage people in our communities. How do leaders set a vision for citizens who are not interested in the greater common good and, instead, are focused on looking after their own interests first? How do leaders keep a country together when society is breaking into more and more factions, and free trade zones increase the power of international corporations to lead while reducing the power of local governments and their constitutions to do so? When half the eligible population fails to vote, how do leaders design programs for the *whole* versus the vocal, very small minority?

This is where *meaning* comes in. Good leaders are those who are open to involving others in shared debate and authentic dialogue to develop a collective vision and redefine the role and structure of government. Good leaders persuade people to sacrifice for the common good. Good leaders synthesize other people's positions, they do not criticize them. Good leaders inspire people to fulfill their potential, which in turn enables society to fulfill its potential. But how should we define "success" in society? Too often, we are focused on growth as measured by GDP (gross domestic product), defined as the value of economic activity. Governments become obsessed with programs that hold promise to boost GDP on the never-ending quest for more growth by increasing the consumption of goods and services.

The problem with this approach is that GDP is not a good measure of the actual well-being or general welfare of a society. GDP fails to take into account the meaningful life—connecting meaningfully with others (including our relationships and caring for our communities and environments), engaging with deeper purpose (including our level of education, the sharing economy, and volunteer efforts), and embracing life with attitude (including the state of our mental, spiritual, and physical health). Should success not be measured by other means, such as in Bhutan, where they measure "gross national happiness"? With meaning at its core, the new economy should value these broader human factors, not just the traditional material and financial factors that are usually associated with measuring GDP.

One challenge facing society-at-large is unemployment. Unemployment is a meaning issue as well as a money issue. Employment is essential to well-being. People need the dignity of everyday work, a purpose to get up in the morning, and the self-esteem that comes with contributing to a worthy goal. Unfortunately, modern society faces an onslaught of automation and artificial intelligence (AI), which will likely lead to more unemployment in the future. As more and more companies automate jobs in order to cut costs, routine tasks and the human beings associated with them are being replaced by technology. Here are some examples:

- Robots are doing more factory work.
- Kiosks with touch screens take customer orders at restaurants (making it difficult to even get a job at McDonald's).
- Kiosks at airports check people in for their flights.
- Sales people are replaced with online ordering from home computers or smartphones.
- Call centers are automated.
- Health care assessments, such as radiology, are diagnosed by technology.
- Mail is sorted by machine, not by hand.

- E-books replace the need to print, inventory, transport, and sell books in retail stores, replacing workers all along the way.
- Uber, Airbnb, and Hotels.com replace travel agents with technology.
- Customers scan their own purchases at stores, replacing checkout clerks.
- Teachers are replaced by centralized, online courses.
- "Block chain" technology eliminates office jobs and enables global transactions to occur, bypassing many of the standard systems and workers in these systems.

Technology is driving massive global unemployment, wiping out jobs at all levels, and increasing inequality. No longer is there long-term job security. When unemployment increases, instability in our society increases. We need to ask how technology, specifically AI, will contribute to us living a *meaningful* life. If we turn everything (or even just half of our jobs) over to technology, what will our society look like in the future? This is not simply a question about the future of technology, the job market, or macroeconomics. On the contrary, it is a question of profound *existential* concern since it pertains to the fate of humanity and the world.

We need to help people prepare for the future. Unfortunately, many of our educational institutions are busy teaching about the past rather than equipping people, regardless of age, with the mind-set and skills necessary to succeed in the future. Instead of teaching solely what was and what is, we should balance educational offerings by also teaching what *could be.* If we believe our society will be a leader in innovation and entrepreneurship, we should change the education systems to support this vision. We should stress that education is a lifelong process, not strictly the domain of people in certain age categories. To be a truly meaningful and transformative path to personal, organizational, and societal wellbeing, education in its ideal form needs to be *interdisciplinary* in its design, process, and outcomes.

A unique initiative in Greece offers the kind of education attributes we are talking about—one with which, in the spirit of full disclosure, we have personal experience as faculty and advisers. The International Center for Leading Studies (TICLS), based in Athens, is an independent, nonprofit foundation, dedicated to preparing people for the future and advancing intercultural awareness and collaboration through authentic dialogue. Offering nontraditional, experiential, interdisciplinary, multicultural, continuing education programs for all age groups (high school and university students, young and senior professionals), the aim of TICLS is "to promote emotionally intelligent society leadership with values through programs that disseminate information, stimulate dialogue, broaden personal horizons, expand knowledge, encourage inter-cultural dialogue, and challenge perspectives across our intertwined world."[10]

The Interdisciplinary Leadership Academy, one of TICLS's summer programs, for instance, offers university students from around the world an innovative academic experience designed "to develop a geopolitical culture for participants, elucidate the complex nature of modern international economy, and develop soft skills, such as diplomacy, communication, and relationship building." According to TICLS dean and cofounder, Dr. Aliki Mitsakos, MD, PhD, "TICLS creates educational programs that complement formal education by focusing on the latest trends in the world around us . . . trends changing the landscape in dozens of ways—politically, socially, economically. . . . education, in its primal meaning, that will enhance the Leadership potential of the participating individuals and the ancient Greek concept of a complete personality, *Paedeia.*"

To be sure, the educational opportunities that TICLS provides are unique and, in our opinion, offer an inspirational model of education reform that can and needs to be applied on a global scale. Not all education programs, of course, are as innovative. Very few schools offer classes in innovation as a subject area, either within or across disciplines. When we taught innovation management at the University of Toronto, our course was one of the few in North America to challenge students to develop a broader view of the world, to identify emerging trends and innovative opportunities, and to think through challenges with innovative thinking techniques. As technology is forcing all of us to redefine opportunities, jobs, and processes, we need to develop new skills, including many that are still referred to as "soft skills."

We need to put *meaning* at the core of education. What separates us, as human beings, from technology is meaning. The more technology we have, the more meaning we need. We need to emphasize skills, along the lines of TICLS, like creative thinking, leadership, collaboration, empathy, networking, diplomacy, and persuasive selling. We need to include more personal development and meaning-focused courses in our schools at all levels, so that students can deepen their understanding of themselves and their natural talents. Many students graduate with lots of knowledge *except* in the key area of "know thyself!" This shortcoming in our education systems must change. A greater emphasis on meaning (that is, putting "meaning at the core") can help at the individual level. It can also create a stronger sense of community and society.

Embrace Life with Attitude (A)

Viktor Frankl taught us that if we look for it, there is a seed of meaning in every moment of our lives. Unfortunately, we often overlook and thus don't discover this meaning because we focus instead on all the stress we are experiencing in the various areas of our lives. We look outward to our friends, neighbors, and coworkers and see that they, too, are struggling with stress. We turn on the television or go online and see that people all over the world are suffering. It becomes a vicious cycle: the more we experience a sense of instability in our communities and in the world at large, the more stress and existential angst we experience. We can break out of this vicious cycle by finding the "seeds of meaning" in our own lives and work. This discovery process is aided by connecting meaningfully with others, engaging with deeper purpose, and embracing life with an appreciative attitude. We can also turn to others for support, for we are not in this life alone.

Two main areas of stress in our society are finances and health. If we put meaning at the core of our finances, we might be able to deal with some of the stresses people face by helping them manage their money better. Banks and other financial institutions, including credit card companies, auto and student loan providers, can do so much more in educating people about making smarter choices about the debt they undertake. Perhaps, as a result, they will learn (and be encouraged) to avoid the pressures to consume more "stuff," which typically creates yet another vicious cycle of debt. If we put meaning at the core of our health, we might be able to turn the tide against obesity, emotional distress, and disease; instead, we could focus on the state of our health and the overall state of our well-being. Medical doctors and other health-care practitioners can be encouraged to teach us about health before inflammation and disease occur. A stronger focus on the meaning of nutrition, mental health, and healthy lifestyle choices can help improve our lives, including addressing the root causes of addictions, depression, and even aggression—what Frankl called the "mass neurotic triad" (introduced in chapter 4). The sooner we learn to make meaning the core driver of all our thoughts, feelings, and actions, the healthier we might be.

It all starts with meaning. When we live and work from the core of meaning, we can understand how the pieces of our lives fit together and perhaps improve the contributions we can make to society. As Steve Jobs and his company Apple encouraged us to do in the famous 1997 marketing campaign, we need to "think different." Jobs and his colleagues believed that people with passion can really change the world. They profiled the crazies—people like Richard Branson, Neil Armstrong, Albert Einstein, and Rosa Parks—people crazy enough to believe they could change the world and did! Importantly, none of these pioneers and thought leaders could have accomplished what they did had it not been for their resilient, can-do attitude. This was a choice that each individual, against all odds, had to make on his or her own; no one could have done it for them.

To be sure, times have changed since 1997. Never before have so many ordinary people had the capacity to be *extraordinary* and change the world. All of us need to ask ourselves if we believe we can change the world *and* if we can "think different" to be the change we'd like to see. We need to ask ourselves if our choice of attitude will allow us to realize our dreams. Will our attitude propel us forward or hold us back? Remember Frankl's timeless advice: "Where there is a will, there is a way; I add, where there is an aim, there is a will." Do we have such an aim, specifically one that will allow us to manifest our *will to meaning*? In this context, what role(s) do we want to play in creating more *meaningful* workplaces, more *meaningful* communities, and a kinder, more generous, more *meaning*-centered society?

Meaning is at the heart of what makes us human. But we cannot heal our workplaces and society unless we first heal ourselves. Ultimately, as we've suggested throughout this book, each of us holds the keys to our inner mental prison cell. Consequently, we each have the authority and the ability, should we decide to exercise them, to release ourselves from our captivity and no longer be prisoners of our thoughts. When we understand the sources of meaning in our own lives, we open up pathways to unlimited opportunities for improving our resilience and engagement, advance our health and well-being, and increase our performance and innovation in all aspects of living and working. Put differently, we can use meaning as the foundation for all we do in life, work, and society. With meaning at the core, we can contribute to building a world that really works for all!

Meaning Reflections

Meaning Moment Exercise Imagine an ideal society that was designed and operated with meaning at its core. What would it look like? Describe how it would be different from the society you live in today. Now think about ways in which you can help your neighborhood or local community change or develop in ways that resemble what you have envisioned for the ideal society. In what way(s) might you involve your family members, friends, and coworkers in helping to accomplish this vision of a neighborhood or local community that has meaning at its core?

Meaning Questions

- What kind deed or act of kindness did you do today to "pay it forward"?
- How has your work improved the lives of others? How can your work improve the lives of others in the future?
- Does your attitude propel you forward or hold you back from contributing meaningfully to society?

Meaning Affirmation

I will authentically commit to making a positive, meaningful difference in the world through my attitude, words, and actions.

Viktor Frankl's Legacy Continues

*The salvation of man is through love and in love. I under-
stood how a man who has nothing left in this world
still may know bliss, be it only for a brief moment, in
the contemplation of his beloved.*[1] (V. Frankl)

It has been twenty years since I (Alex) met with Dr. Frankl at
his home in Vienna, Austria, and after proposing the idea of
writing this book, he grabbed my arm and encouragingly said,
"Alex, yours is the book that needs to be written." It is perhaps even more significant to note that 2017 marks the twen-
tieth year since Frankl's passing in 1997. A truly exceptional
human being, Viktor Frankl will forever bring light to darkness
along the path and guide the human quest for meaning. Psychologist Dr. Jeffrey Zeig, who was privileged to know Frankl
and his family, anchored his sentiments about the influence
of Frankl in words taken from Albert Camus's *The First Man*:
"There are people who vindicate the world, who help others
just by their presence." Without a doubt, Frankl was a man

whose very presence vindicated the world. His legacy continues to be one of hope and possibility. He saw the human condition at its worst, with people behaving in unimaginably intolerable ways. He also saw human beings rising to heights of compassion and caring in what can only be described as miraculous acts of unselfishness and transcendence.

Indeed, Frankl leaves a profound legacy. Through his life and work, he reminds us that we all have important work to do, that whatever we do is important, and that meaning can be found everywhere, all the time. In this chapter it is our intent to highlight some of the ways in which Frankl's legacy continues to influence (and change) lives, work, and society. Against the backdrop of his extraordinary life and timeless wisdom, may Viktor Frankl's memory be eternal.

Changing Lives

Frankl developed and practiced Logotherapy and Existential Analysis as a way for everyone—from death row inmates and concentration-camp survivors to CEOs, bus drivers, and postmodern philosophy professors—to find and open the doors of rooms of despair. His framework of being and doing offered an entirely new design for our lives. He provided a disciplined approach for discovering meaning in even the most catastrophic of circumstances—an approach rooted firmly in his profound personal experience.

In this regard, Frankl's influence cannot be overestimated. Indeed, it transcends a single lifetime and manifests itself in many different ways, on multiple levels. For those of us who were fortunate to have been in his presence, the experience, without doubt, was transformative. However, his "presence" and influence have been—and continue to be—felt by far more people around the world because of the words of wisdom that he has shared through his writings. It is nearly impossible to find someone who hasn't been affected in a profound way after having read Frankl's Man's Search for Meaning. "That book changed my life," so many people in all walks and stages of life have told us. Indeed, it is no wonder that the Library of Congress named Man's Search for Meaning one of the ten most influential books in America. Although we agree that this is a well-deserved honor, the book's influence goes far beyond the United States!

Dr. Frankl's writing has affected people from all walks of life—educators, students, religious leaders (including Pope Paul VI), politicians, philosophers, psychologists, psychiatrists, and millions of others in search of meaning in their own lives. Yet he was humble, modest, and not interested in promoting himself in the fashion of the times. He was also inspirational to those whose lives were anchored in struggle. For example, Jerry Long, a young man from Texas, was a victim of a tragic diving accident. Although Long was left a quadriplegic, he was determined to become a psychologist because he liked people and wanted to help them. As a college freshman, Long read Frankl's book, Man's Search for Meaning, and found new insights every time he read the book. Despite being able to type only by using a pencil-sized rod that he held in his mouth, Long wrote to Frankl, remarking that his own difficulties seemed to be far less than those suffered by Frankl and his comrades in the concentration camps. When Long eventually met Frankl in person, he told him: "The accident broke my back, but it did not break me."[2]

Despite his severe handicap, Jerry Long was able to fulfill his goal of becoming a psychologist, earning his doctorate in clinical psychology in 1990. Dr. Jerry L. Long Jr., who died in 2004, was an extraordinary, inspirational figure and, as Dr. Frankl rightly observed, was a living testimony to "the defiant power of the Spirit." Long had always believed: "I have suffered but I know that, without the suffering, the growth I have achieved would not have been possible." He wrote:

> *Once, after speaking to a large audience, I was asked if I ever felt sad because I could no longer walk. I replied, "Professor Frankl can hardly see, I cannot walk at all, and many of you can hardly cope with life. What is crucial to remember is this—we don't need just our eyes, just our legs, or just our minds. All we need are the wings of our souls and together we can fly."*[3]

References to Frankl's work are numerous. Best-selling author Stephen R. Covey, who wrote *The 7 Habits of Highly Effective People* and the foreword to this book, was particularly influenced by Frankl's vision. In their book *First Things First: To Live, to Love, to Learn, to Leave a Legacy*, Covey and his associates referred to Frankl's concentration camp experiences and cited the following passage from Frankl's *Man's Search for Meaning*: "The single most important factor, he realized, was a sense of future vision—the impelling conviction of those who were to survive was that they had a mission to perform, some important work left to do."[4]

Extending the Discipline

Frankl did not promote himself or his school of thought and practice like many other pioneers and leaders in his field. However, his legacy, in large part, has been driven by his disciples and other loyal followers. In this regard, what is referred to as the "Third Viennese School of Psychotherapy" (the predecessors being the Freudian and Adlerian Schools) consists of two disciplinary parts: Logotherapy, the meaning-centered therapeutic practice, and Existential Analysis, the philosophical foundation of the meaning-centered approach. Frankl's expertise in both psychiatry and philosophy, coupled with his extraordinary life experiences, made him ideally suited for what became his meaning "ministry."

In 1992 the Viktor Frankl Institute was established in Vienna, Austria.[5] Today the Institute continues to serve as the center of a worldwide network of research and training institutes and societies dedicated to maintaining and fostering the lifework of Viktor Frankl, including advancing his philosophy and therapeutic system of Logotherapy and Existential Analysis. There are more than one hundred institutions around the world, representing over forty countries, that are accredited members of the International Association of Logotherapy and Existential Analysis at the Viktor Frankl Institute Vienna. The Institute also provides accreditation/certification of individual Logotherapists in different professional fields (for example, physicians, clinical psychologists, psychotherapists, counselors, and coaches).

In addition to supporting academic degree programs and external research projects, the Institute collaborates with the City of Vienna's Viktor Frankl Fund to grant scholarships and award prizes for work in the field of meaning-centered humanistic psychotherapy. It also has exclusive access to Frankl's private archives and the world's largest collection of texts and research on Logotherapy and Existential Analysis.

As part of its rigorous agenda, the Institute organizes a Biennial International Congress on the Future of Logotherapy, held in Vienna. We were honored that Alex was one of the featured speakers at the 2016 Congress, especially since he shared the stage with some of Logotherapy's most prominent practitioners and advocates, including Viktor Frankl's beloved wife, Dr. Eleonore (Elly) Frankl.

The global reach and influence of the Viktor Frankl Institute and its worldwide affiliates continue to increase due, in part, to a growing presence on various social media platforms as well as from new digital and communication technologies that make the Institute's work more readily available. It is noteworthy to see attention to meaning-centered humanistic psychotherapy and existential analysis, as well as references to Frankl's life and legacy, increase in the professional (both academic and practitioner) literature and in mainstream consumer publications.[6]

Crossover Applications

The increasing attention to Frankl's contributions to humanizing psychotherapy and improving the human condition doesn't stop within the professional disciplines that typically are associated with such aims. Because the search for meaning has been shown to be a pertinent concern across all age groups, we have observed many applications, including adaptations, of Frankl's work enter and essentially intersect with other domains.[7] Recent developments in the field of existential psychology and existential therapy increasingly have come to rely on Frankl's philosophical perspective and therapeutic approach. Likewise, fresh insights into what is referred to as "Positive Psychology 2.0" or Second Wave Positive Psychology have opened up new windows of opportunity for applying meaning-centered concepts and practices, specifically Logotherapy and Existential Analysis, and introducing Frankl's wisdom. Psychologist and researcher Dr. Paul T. P. Wong, founder of the International Network on Personal Meaning and our friend and colleague, has been a thought leader in this area.[8]

Crossing over from the therapeutic arena, we are beginning to see Frankl's meaning-centered ideas enter the coaching field. Driven, it seems, by the commonalities as well as the inherent tensions between these two professional tracks—that is, "therapy" vis-à-vis "coaching"—some kind of convergence seems inevitable. In this connection we've observed such developments as existential therapy adding an "existential coaching" dimension to its repertoire, and the professional practice of Cognitive Behavioral Therapy extending its reach into "cognitive behavioral coaching" with the blessing of the International Coach Federation.[9] To be sure, these are significant developments, for they point the way to even more opportunities for Frankl's wisdom with his focus on the human quest for meaning to be seeded and take root in complementary fields of endeavor.

As the theme of this book reveals, the search for meaning in work-related contexts has also grown in importance since both employers and employees within organizations, as well as all other kinds of "workers," are coming to the realization that meaning at the core of their work has benefits that go far beyond conventional metrics of return on investment (ROI) and the financial bottom line. More and more scientific research, including that which we are conducting in MEANINGology under the auspices of the Global Meaning Institute, documents that meaning drives engagement and resilience, health and well-being, and performance and innovation—all characteristics that are fundamental to the working environment.[10] The need to continue to humanize work and the workplace is a quest in and of itself; the meaning paradigm and formula that Viktor Frankl espoused (as do we) not only underscore the importance of this quest but also provide practical, empirically grounded guidelines for pursuing it successfully.

Earlier in this book, especially in chapter 12, we emphasized that government is an important target of opportunity for bringing meaning into the workplace and, at a societal level, into the formulation of public policy. Statements like "It's close enough for government work" and "Innovation in government is an oxymoron" are indictments of those employed by the public service and reflections of ourselves as citizens.[11] The search for meaning at work, including that derived from government service, has moved to center stage and the need to reflect on the meaning of work is perhaps greater today than ever before. Political posturing aside, the time has come to elevate and, in our view, return government service to its position as a noble calling. Managing the public's business, which includes the political realm, deserves no less.[12]

In this regard, we are seeing a growing interest in, and even a new consciousness about, finding meaning in and at work and building meaning-centered workplaces across sectors and industries. We mentioned in chapter 11 that the

Academy of Management (AoM) chose "Making Organizations Meaningful" as its 2016 annual conference theme. Among its various and related interest groups, AoM has a Public and Nonprofit Division that certainly will benefit from addressing the annual theme and, we hope, will seek to see it continue and expand in the future. Moreover, we've had the occasion to introduce Viktor Frankl and his work to government workers in collaboration with the American Society for Public Administration (ASPA), the largest and most prominent professional association dedicated to advancing excellence in public service, not just in the United States but also on a global scale through its professional development program offerings and publications.

The growing interest in meaning, including Viktor Frankl's work and our own, in all kinds of organizations and work is clearly evident. We should mention that *Prisoners of Our Thoughts* was even referenced by the online *New World Encyclopedia* in the "legacy" section of the encyclopedia's entry on Viktor Frankl! In particular, we are credited with predicting that Frankl's contributions to health and wellness, as well as to "good" government and business, would be profound.[13]

Popular Culture

Viktor Frankl's name and ideas are also finding their way with increasing regularity into popular culture—on television, radio, magazines, newspapers, and, yes, even in movies. Frankl and his work have appeared in such mainstream consumer publications as *Psychology Today* and India's premiere lifestyle magazine, *Complete Wellbeing*. In 2015 it was announced that Frankl's best seller, Man's Search for Meaning, was finally heading for the big screen as a feature film.[14] Fuego Films has teamed up with Emmy Award–winning journalist Giselle Fernandez to secure the film-option rights to the book, which had been held back until Frankl's estate made the deal. Screenwriter Adam Gibgot has been given the honor of writing the script based on the book. Our friend Mary Cimiluca, who represents the Frankl estate and who also is a filmmaker, will be an executive producer on this exciting project. According to Gibgot, "The movie is about the best and worst of humanity, but how out of the worst the best can emerge."

Jimmy Fallon, host of NBC's Tonight Show, has played a recent role in exposing the public to Viktor Frankl and his insights. In the summer of 2015, Fallon had an accident in which he fell at home and nearly lost one of his fingers.[15] The injury required six hours of microsurgery and required Fallon to stay in the intensive care unit of New York's Bellevue Hospital for ten days. As Fallon described it to his television audience when he returned to work after two weeks off, he started "losing it halfway through" his hospital stay. At his physician's recommendation, he began to read books about the meaning of life and, in particular, Frankl's Man's Search for Meaning. On live television Fallon said that he "absolutely loved it," and he displayed a copy of the book. He also said that he "highlighted quotes and things. I e-mailed all my friends. I'm like, 'Dude, you have to read this book—I know the meaning of life.'"[16] On a more serious note, Fallon shared the following insights about what he had learned from his ordeal and, consequently, from Viktor Frankl:

This is the meaning of my life. I belong on TV. I should be talking to people who are watching, who are either in an ICU— wherever you are, at home—if anyone is suffering at all, this is my job. I'm here to make you laugh. I'm here to make you have a good time. . . . That's my job. That's why I'm here. I want to spread the love.[17]

Eternal Message

The memory of Viktor Frankl, as we said at the beginning of this chapter, is eternal. So is Frankl's inspirational and aspirational message of meaning. Here we briefly describe three initiatives that, in different ways, will guarantee that the memory of his life and legacy is never lost.[18]

Viktor & I. In the fascinating and beautifully crafted documentary film *Viktor & I*, Dr. Frankl's grandson and filmmaker, Alexander Vesely, gives a unique and personal look at his famous grandfather about whom he coined the moniker "Pioneer of Meaning." The film is based on interviews with Frankl's friends and colleagues from around the world that were conducted over a three-year period. Among Vesely's aims was to discover and depict how Frankl's theories were connected to him as a person. *Viktor & I* shows Frankl as he was seen by relatives, friends, colleagues, students, and acquaintances in various professional and private settings. "We can witness a variety of encounters and anecdotes— from funny to profound, from sentimental to inspiring— but always full of insight into a most human, and humane, personality."[19]

Viktor Frankl Museum. On March 26, 2015, on the occasion of what would have been Viktor Frankl's 110th birthday, the grand opening of the world's first Viktor Frankl

Museum was held in Vienna, Austria.[20] The Museum is an initiative of the Viktor Frankl Center Vienna (Viktor Frankl Zentrum Wien), which operates in cooperation with the Viktor Frankl Institute and a number of allied entities in Austria. The Museum was designed to be an experiential, interactive, sensory, and multimedia learning opportunity for visitors to become introduced to Frankl's life, his philosophy, and his approach to psychotherapy. Visitors are invited to immerse themselves in Frankl's meaning-centered teachings and to deal with personal questions of meaning and existence. The overall aim of the Viktor Frankl Center is to preserve and disseminate Frankl's lifework in all spheres of society as well as to integrate the basic ideas of Logotherapy and Existential Analysis into such applied disciplines as medicine, psychotherapy, philosophy, education, and economics through a wide variety of programs and services. Professionals, students, and the general public can get acquainted with Frankl's body of work through courses, seminars, workshops, lectures, literature, and film, among other educational options.

Statue of Responsibility. Viktor Frankl warned that freedom threatens to degenerate into mere license and arbitrariness unless it is lived in terms of responsibleness. Although he enjoyed his time in America and admired much about it, Frankl was not shy about criticizing the popular understanding of some cherished American values, such as our notion of freedom. He took exception, for instance, to what appeared to be a commonly accepted view of equating freedom with a license to do virtually anything one wants. To Frankl, freedom without responsibility was an oxymoron. That is why he recommended that the Statue of Liberty on Liberty Island in

New York Harbor be complemented by a Statue of Responsibility somewhere along the West Coast.

Freedom, however, is not the last word. Freedom is only part of the story and half of the truth. Freedom is but the negative aspect of the whole phenomenon whose positive aspect is responsibleness. In fact, freedom is in danger of degenerating into mere arbitrariness unless it is lived in terms of responsibleness. That is why I recommend that the Statue of Liberty on the East Coast be supplemented by a Statue of Responsibility on the West Coast.[21]
(V. Frankl)

We've always been intrigued by Dr. Frankl's idea for a Statue of Responsibility. Such a monument makes sense to us and, in our opinion, would be much more than just a bookend to the Statue of Liberty. It could serve, among other things, as an important reminder of what is required to safeguard true freedom and a democratic way of life. Moreover, it would be an extraordinary way to celebrate Frankl's life and legacy. It would be a meaningful, everlasting symbol of his contributions to humankind.

A nonprofit foundation exists to advance Frankl's idea with the goal of completing the statue, which would be a three-hundred-foot national monument, complete with a large event venue similar to the National Mall in Washington, DC, somewhere on the West Coast by the year 2020.[22] A model of the proposed Statue of Responsibility, consisting of a pair of clasped hands oriented vertically, has been designed by commissioned sculptor Gary Lee Price. The model is being used to help raise private funds for the project, which is estimated to cost between $300 million and $400 million. It is interesting to note that the late Stephen R. Covey, who wrote the foreword to *Prisoners of Our Thoughts*, was a member of the original committee formed by Viktor Frankl in the 1990s to bring the concept of the Statue of Responsibility to life.

The Force Awakens

Indeed, the spirit of Viktor Frankl lives on, and his ageless wisdom about the human quest for meaning continues to spread around the world. More people in all stages and walks of life are being given the opportunity to benefit from Frankl's wisdom through new channels, such as via new media and social networks, and are revealing their hunger for something "more" in life, work, and society than what they have experienced or can envision for their future. "The times they are a-changin'," sang Bob Dylan. We consider the meaning movement that is happening to be a megatrend of the twenty-first century. In a postmodern world characterized by increasing complexity, insecurity, uncertainty, and inequality, yet surrounded by unappreciated, unused, and, in many cases, hoarded abundance, the call—the "cry"—for meaning can be heard loud and clear. Yes, Bob Dylan, the times are changing and rightly so. To paraphrase a line from the best-selling Italian novel *The Leopard* (*Il Gattopardo*), "If you want things to stay the same, then something is going to have to change."

By living a life with meaning right to his last breath, Frankl showed us how his existential philosophy and therapeutic approach were grounded in practice. His personal experiences throughout his long life, both as a survivor of the Nazi death camps and as a revered and respected thought leader, illuminate the unlimited potential of a human being.

Frankl's life gives us rich and ample evidence that the keys to freedom from life's prison cells—real and imagined—are within us, and within reach. Meaning, as Dr. Frankl taught us, can be found everywhere—in and through all of life's experiences. Like energy, it cannot be created or destroyed, only transformed. It exists in the moment—in all moments—and is only waiting to be discovered.

All things being equal, we suspect that the new "balanced scorecard" of the twenty-first century will be concerned more with success at making a life than with success at making a living. As people become increasingly aware of their mortality and their commitment to meaningful values and goals—that is, their *will to meaning*—they become more likely to consider the kind of personal legacy they would like to leave behind. This shift in consciousness will keep them on their path to meaning. In the end, the "good life," as the ancient Greek philosophers wisely espoused, is not about the search for happiness, it is about the search for *meaning*. But discovering meaning in life and work is both a personal and collective responsibility—a message you have heard numerous times throughout this book.

For this to happen, we must make an authentic commitment not to forget the core message of *why* meaning is so important, *how* meaning can benefit all aspects of our lives, and *what* we must do to discover meaning. This is the core message that Viktor Frankl was seeking to convey, share with the world, and leave behind as *his* personal legacy. Remember the eloquent words of Stephen Covey in his foreword: "To learn something but not to do is really not to learn. To know something but not to do is really not to know." To bring meaning into our lives requires learning, knowing, and then doing. Importantly, this kind of authentic, action-oriented learning and knowing cannot happen until we are no longer prisoners of our thoughts.

Meaning Reflections

Meaning Moment Exercise Think about how Viktor Frankl's life and legacy, including what you've learned about his System of Logotherapy and Existential Analysis, can help you deal with challenges in your life and work, now and in the future. What ideas, life lessons, and/or Logotherapeutic principles do you feel will be most useful—and meaningful—to you? How will you demonstrate that you understand and are authentically committed to practicing these principles in your everyday life and work?

Meaning Questions

- In what ways do the underlying values and goals in your life and work reflect Frankl's *will to meaning*?
- What can and will you do to share Frankl's inspirational meaning message with others?
- How can you help family members, friends, and coworkers find meaning in their lives and work using what you've learned about and from Frankl?

Meaning Affirmation

In the spirit of Viktor Frankl's work and legacy, I will pursue meaning in my life, my work, and in our broader society.

Notes

Chapter 1

1. Viktor E. Frankl, *Man's Search for Meaning: An Introduction to Logotherapy*, 4th ed. (Boston: Beacon, 1992), 113–14.
2. Viktor E. Frankl, *The Unconscious God* (New York: Washington Square, 1975), 120.
3. Viktor E. Frankl, *Recollections: An Autobiography* (New York: Plenum, 1997), 53.
4. Frankl, *Man's Search for Meaning*, 75.
5. Frankl, *Man's Search for Meaning*, 108.
6. Viktor E. Frankl, lecture, delivered February 18, 1963, Religion in Education Foundation, University of Illinois. See also Viktor E. Frankl, *Psychotherapy and Existentialism* (New York: Washington Square, 1967), 147.
7. Frankl, *Psychotherapy and Existentialism*, 4, emphasis added.
8. Frankl, *Man's Search for Meaning*, 49.

Chapter 2

1. Frankl, *Autobiography*, 35.
2. Frankl, *Autobiography*, 19. See also Anna S. Redsand, *Viktor Frankl: A Life Worth Living* (New York: Clarion Books, 2006).
3. See, for example, Alex N. Pattakos, "Searching for the Soul of Government," in *Rediscovering the Soul of Business: A Renaissance of Values*, edited by Bill DeFoore and John Renesch, 321–23 (San Francisco: New Leaders Press, 1995). Frankl's choice of the Greek word *logos*, including its spiritual underpinnings, in the naming of his school of psychotherapy was discussed in a personal conversation with Alex Pattakos, Vienna, Austria, August 6, 1996. For further evidence of Frankl's intention to use the word in its spiritual sense,

see Viktor E. Frankl, *The Doctor and the Soul: From Psychotherapy to Logotherapy* (New York: Random House, 1986), xvii.

4. David Winston, *Logos and Mystical Theology in Philo of Alexandria* (Cincinnati: Hebrew Union College Press, 1985). This kind of interpretation of *logos* received attention more recently in Karen Armstrong's best seller *A History of God*, in which she notes that Saint John had made it clear that Jesus was the *Logos* and, moreover, that the *Logos* was God.

5. Frankl, *Autobiography*, 53

6. Frankl, *Autobiography*, 98.

7. Frankl, *Man's Search for Meaning*, 75.

8. See also Frankl, *Man's Search for Meaning*, 117.

9. Frankl, *Autobiography*, 53.

Chapter 3

1. Frankl, *Man's Search for Meaning*, 75.

2. Personal conversation with Alex Pattakos, Vienna, Austria, August 6, 1996. See also Viktor E. Frankl, keynote address delivered at the Evolution of Psychotherapy Conference, Anaheim, California, December 12–16, 1990.

3. I am indebted to Dr. Myron S. Augsburger for this account. See also Nelson Mandela, *Long Walk to Freedom* (New York: Little, Brown, 1995).

4. Christopher Reeve, *Still Me* (New York: Ballantine Books, 1999), 267.

5. Interview with Christopher Reeve on *Larry King Live*, originally aired on February 22, 1996.

6. Reeve, *Still Me*, 3–4, emphasis added.

7. See Christopher Reeve, *Nothing Is Impossible: Reflections on a New Life* (New York: Random House, 2002). See also Dana Reeve, *Care Packages: Letters to Christopher Reeve from Strangers and Other Friends* (New York: Random House, 1999).

8. Frankl, keynote address delivered at the Evolution of Psychotherapy Conference, Anaheim, California, December 12–16, 1990.

9. Frankl, *Psychotherapy and Existentialism*, 3.

Chapter 4

1. Frankl, *Man's Search for Meaning*, 87–88.

2. Frankl, *Man's Search for Meaning*, 105.

3. Viktor E. Frankl, *The Unheard Cry for Meaning* (New York: Washington Square, 1978), 21.
4. This ministry of meaning has continued to manifest itself beyond Chappell's efforts to ensure that Tom's of Maine, which became part of the Colgate-Palmolive Company in 2006, maintains its core values, beliefs, and mission as a business enterprise. Tom and Kate Chappell's newest venture, Rambler's Way Farm, continues their passion for creating superior products for a sustainable lifestyle, while at the same time creating a business that can be a positive force for its consumers, workers, communities, and the planet. Rambler's Way Farm is "a company that pays homage to America's rich history as a textile producer, while breathing new life into the domestic wool industry, through our collaboration with farmers and producers around the country." See http://www.ramblersway.com/toms.
5. Rodney Crowell, "Time to Go Inward," *Fate's Right Hand* (Sony Music Entertainment, 2003). We're indebted to our friend and colleague Stewart Levine for introducing us to Rodney Crowell's music and lyrics. Some people, even though they can clearly see such prison bars, are unwilling to go inward and do something constructive about what they see. Take, for example, former major league baseball player and manager Pete Rose, whose gambling addiction, a manifestation of the will to pleasure, proved to be his own demise, as he describes in his autobiography *My Prison Without Bars* (New York: Rodale Books, 2004).
6. Viktor E. Frankl, *The Will to Meaning*, 1985 lecture (available on tape from Zeig, Tucker & Theisen, Phoenix, ISBN: 1-932462-08-2). See also Viktor E. Frankl, *The Will to Meaning: Foundations and Applications of Logotherapy* (New York: Penguin Books, 1988).
7. "The Classroom of the Future," *Newsweek*, October 29, 2001, online at http://www.newsweek.com/classroom-future-154191.

Chapter 5
1. Frankl, *Man's Search for Meaning*, 114.
2. Frankl, *Man's Search for Meaning*, 115.
3. See, for example, Phil Jackson and Hugh Delehanty, *Sacred Hoops: Spiritual Lessons of a Hardwood Warrior* (New York: Hyperion, 1995).
4. Frankl, keynote address, delivered at the Evolution of Psychotherapy Conference, Anaheim, California, December 12–16, 1990.
5. Frankl, *Man's Search for Meaning*, 107.
6. Frankl, *The Doctor and the Soul*, xix.

7. We're indebted to Art Jackson for introducing us to this particular exercise.

8. Frankl, *Unheard Cry*, 45.

Chapter 6

1. Frankl, *Man's Search for Meaning*, 125.

2. Frankl, *The Doctor and the Soul*, 118.

3. Frankl, *The Doctor and the Soul*, 118.

4. See Ronna Lichtenberg, *It's Not Business, It's Personal: The 9 Relationship Principles That Power Career* (New York: Hyperion, 2002).

5. Jean-François Manzoni and Jean-Louis Barsoux, "The Set-Up-to-Fail Syndrome," *Harvard Business Review* (March–April 1998): 101–13.

6. Frankl, *The Doctor and the Soul*, 126.

7. See, for example, Charles C. Manz, *The Power of Failure* (San Francisco: Berrett-Koehler, 2002).

8. Management guru Tom Peters as cited in Robert Johnson, "Speakers Use Failure to Succeed," *Toronto Globe and Mail*, January 30, 2001.

9. Frankl, *The Doctor and the Soul*, 224.

10. Haddon Klingberg, *When Life Calls Out to Us: The Love and Lifework of Viktor and Elly Frankl* (New York: Doubleday, 2001), 67. See also Frankl, *The Doctor and the Soul*, 232.

11. The bookkeeper's story as told in Frankl, *Man's Search for Meaning*, 128.

12. Frankl, *Man's Search for Meaning*, 127.

13. Frankl, *Autobiography*, 67–68.

14. Frankl, *The Doctor and the Soul*, 224.

Chapter 7

1. Frankl, *Psychotherapy and Existentialism*, 20.

2. The Dalai Lama and Howard C. Cutler, *The Art of Happiness at Work* (New York: Riverhead Books, 2003), 200.

3. Responses from MBA students to Andy Borowitz's talk at the Wharton School as reported in *USA Today*, August 19, 2003.

4. Rubin Battino, *Meaning: A Play Based on the Life of Viktor E. Frankl* (Williston, VT: Crown House, 2002), 66. See also Frankl, *Man's Search for Meaning*, 54, emphasis added.

5. Charlotte Foltz Jones, *Mistakes That Worked* (New York: Delacorte, 1991).

6. Frankl, *Autobiography*, 98. See also Frankl, keynote address delivered

at the Evolution of Psychotherapy Conference, Anaheim, California, December 12–16, 1990; and Frankl, *Man's Search for Meaning*, 81–82.

Chapter 8

1. Frankl, *The Doctor and the Soul*, 254.
2. Frankl, *The Doctor and the Soul*, 125.
3. Frankl, *The Doctor and the Soul*, 255.
4. See Charles Taylor, *The Ethics of Authenticity* (Cambridge, MA: Harvard University Press, 1991).

Chapter 9

1. Frankl, *Man's Search for Meaning*, 12.
2. Frankl as quoted in Haddon Klingberg, "When Life Calls Out to Us: The Love and Lifework of Viktor and Elly Frankl," speech, Toronto Youth Corps, February 11, 1973, p. 289.
3. Frankl, *Man's Search for Meaning*, 135.
4. Lovemore Mbigi and Jenny Maree, *Ubuntu: The Spirit of African Transformation Management* (Randburg, South Africa: Knowledge Resources, 1997).
5. The story "The Echo" is told in full in Alex Pattakos and Elaine Dundon, *The OPA! Way: Finding Joy & Meaning in Everyday Life & Work* (Dallas, TX: BenBella Books, 2015), 59.
6. Frankl, *Man's Search for Meaning*, 92–93.
7. Peter M. Senge, *The Fifth Discipline* (New York: Currency/Doubleday, 1994), 13.

Chapter 10

1. Frankl, *Man's Search for Meaning*, 105.
2. Viktor E. Frankl, *Psychotherapy and Existentialism* (New York: Washington Square, 1967), 122.
3. Personal conversation with Alex Pattakos, Vienna, Austria, August 6, 1996. See also Frankl, keynote address delivered at the Evolution of Psychotherapy Conference, Anaheim, California, December 12–16, 1990.
4. Michael J. Berland and Douglas E. Schoen, "How the Economic Crisis Changed Us," *Parade*, November 1, 2009, pp. 4–5.
5. Frankl, *Psychotherapy and Existentialism*, 27.
6. "Think Millennials Have It Tough? For Generation K, Life Is Even Harsher," *The Guardian*, March 19, 2016.

7. See Frankl, *The Doctor and the Soul*, 26.
8. See Mabel Sieh, "Life's a Roller Coaster," *South China Morning Post*, April 29, 2013, online at http://yp.scmp.com/article/4979/lifes-roller-coaster.
9. Mark Gerzon, *Coming into Our Own: Understanding the Adult Metamorphosis* (New York: Delacorte, 1992).

Chapter 11

1. Frankl, *The Will to Meaning* (1985 lecture). See also Frankl, *The Will to Meaning: Foundations and Applications of Logotherapy*.
2. See Caleb Melby, "Ellison's Paycheck Is $103 Million and He's Still a Bargain," March 11, 2015, online at http://www.bloomberg.com/news/articles/2015-03-11/ellison-s-103-million-pay-seen-as-a-good-deal-for-shareholders.
3. Gallup Organization, "Engaged Employees Inspire Company Innovation," *Gallup Management Journal*, October 12, 2006.
4. Amy Adkins, "Employee Engagement in U.S. Stagnant in 2015," January 13, 2016, online at http://www.gallup.com/poll/188144/employee-engagement-stagnant-2015.aspx.
5. "One in Two US Employees Looking to Leave or Checked out on the Job, Says New *What's Working*™ Research by Mercer," June 20, 2011, online at http://www.businesswire.com/news/home/20110620005336/en/Employees-Leave-Checked-Job-What%E2%80%99s-Working%E2%84%A2-Research.
6. Steelcase Global Report, *Engagement and the Global Workplace* (Grand Rapids, MI: Steelcase, Inc., 2016), online at http://www.steelcase.com/insights/360-magazine/steelcase-global-report/.
7. For example, see Joanne Richard, "The Toxic Workplace: From Narcissists and Pot-stirrers, to Drama Queens and Bully Bosses, Ultimately Toxic People Can Take Other People Down with Them," October 7, 2015, online at http://www.torontosun.com/2015/10/07/the-toxic-workplace.
8. Gallup Organization, "Engaged Employees Inspire Company Innovation," *Gallup Management Journal*, October 12, 2006.
9. Eileen E. Morrison, George C. Burke, and Lloyd Greene, "Meaning in Motivation: Does Your Organization Need an Inner Life?" Texas State University–San Marcos, Faculty Publications, School of Health Administration, 2007.
10. Victor Lipman, "Key Management Trends for 2016? Here Are 6 Research-Based Predictions," *Forbes*, January 1, 2016,

online at http://www.forbes.com/sites/victorlipman/2016/01/01/
key-management-trends-for-2016-here-are-6-research-based
-predictions/#403e455d1071.

11. See "Satisfaction Beats Salary: Philips Work/Life Survey Finds
American Workers Willing to Take Pay Cut for More Personally
Meaningful Careers," May 17, 2013, online at http://www.news
center.philips.com/us_en/standard/news/press/2013/20130517-Philips
-Work-Life-Survey.wpd#.VXYtVKZ12Ud.

12. Frankl identified three categories of values that, when actualized,
provide sources of meaning: (1) *creative* values (that is, "by doing or
creating something"); (2) *experiential* values (that is, "by experiencing
something or encountering someone"); and (3) *attitudinal* values
(that is, "by choosing one's attitude toward suffering").

13. Donald M. Berwick, *Escape Fire: Designs for the Future of Health
Care* (San Francisco: Jossey-Bass/John Wiley & Sons, 2004), 231,
emphasis added.

14. "Korn Ferry Hay Group Global Study Finds Employee Engagement
at Critically Low Levels," March 31, 2016, online at http://www
.kornferry.com/press/korn-ferry-hay-group-global-study-finds
-employee-engagement-at-critically-low-levels/.

15. Roger Frantz and Alex Pattakos, eds., *Intuition at Work: Pathways to
Unlimited Possibilities* (San Francisco: New Leaders Press, 1996), 4.

16. Anita Roddick, *Body and Soul* (New York: Crown Publishers, 1991).

17. "Analysis of Global EAP Data Reveals Huge Rise in Depression,
Stress, and Anxiety over Past Three Years," *Workplace Options*,
December 16, 2015, online at http://www.workplaceoptions.com/
polls/analysis-of-global-eap-data-reveals-huge-rise-in-depression
-stress-and-anxiety-over-past-three-years/. See also John Hollon, "Last
Word: New Survey Is Clear—More and More Workers Are Stressed
and Depressed," *TLNT | Talent Management and HR*, December 18,
2015, online at http://www.eremedia.com/tlnt/last-word-new-survey
-is-clear-more-and-more-workers-are-stressed-and-depressed/#.

18. See Joe Raelin, "Finding Meaning in the Organization," *MIT Sloan
Management Review* 47, no. 3 (Spring 2006): 64–68.

Chapter 12

1. Frankl, *The Doctor and the Soul*, 130–31.

2. Kalle Lasn and Bruce Grierson, "America the Blue," *Utne Reader
Online*, October 28, 2000.

3. "Food & Coffee 'On Hold' for the Needy," *Greek News Agenda*,

March 1, 2016, online at http://greeknewsagenda.gr/index.php/
topics/culture-society/5881-food-coffee-"on-hold"-for-the-needy.

4. Gregory Pappas, "Vanessa Redgrave: 'The Greek People Are
Showing the World How to be Human, How to Try to Help Fellow
Human Beings,'" *Pappas Post*, January 5, 2016, online at http://www
.pappaspost.com/vanessa-redgrave-the-greek-people-are-showing-the
-world-how-to-be-human-how-to-try-to-help-fellow-human-beings/.

5. Sharon Crowther, "Condo Developers Boost 'Sharing' Features to
Draw Young Buyers," *The Globe and Mail*, March 25, 2016, online at
http://www.theglobeandmail.com/life/home-and-garden/real-estate/
condo-developers-boost-sharing-features-to-draw-young-buyers/
article29385716/.

6. "Korn Ferry Hay Group Global Study Finds Employee Engagement
at Critically Low Levels," March 31, 2016, online at http://www
.kornferry.com/press/korn-ferry-hay-group-global-study-finds
-employee-engagement-at-critically-low-levels/.

7. Thomas Moore, *The Re-Enchantment of Everyday Life* (New York:
HarperCollins, 1996), 126.

8. Hippocrates G. Apostle and Lloyd P. Gerson, *Aristotle's Politics*
(Grinnell, Iowa: The Peripatetic Press, 1986), Book Γ, 84–86.

9. Alex Pattakos, "The Search for Meaning in Government Service,"
Public Administration Review 64, no. 1 (2004): 106.

10. See the International Center for Leading Studies of Athens, Greece,
at http://www.ticls.org/.

Chapter 13

1. Frankl, *Man's Search for Meaning*, 49.

2. Frankl, *Man's Search for Meaning*, 147–49.

3. See the Viktor Frankl Institute at http://www.viktorfrankl.org/e/
long_cv.html.

4. Stephen R. Covey, A. Roger Merrill, and Rebecca R. Merrill, *First
Things First: To Live, to Love, to Learn, to Leave a Legacy* (New York:
Simon & Schuster, 1995), 103.

5. See the Viktor Frankl Institute at http://www.viktorfrankl.org/e/.

6. Such websites as Academia.edu (https://www.academia.edu/) and
ResearchGate (https://www.researchgate.net/) contain numerous
references to pertinent resources in the professional and academic
literature dealing with this topic. In this regard, see Stephen J.
Costello, "Logotherapy as Philosophical Practice," *Philosophical
Practice* 11, no. 1 (March 2016): 1684–1703. For an example of

Viktor Frankl's wisdom in a mainstream consumer publication, see Elaine Dundon and Alex Pattakos, "Why Am I Here? Your Personal Answer to the Ultimate Question," *Complete Wellbeing 9*, no. 1 (2014): 36–46. *Complete Wellbeing* is a leading, award-winning lifestyle magazine in India.

7. Michael F. Steger, Shigehiro Oishi, and Todd B. Kashdan, "Meaning in Life Across the Life Span: Levels and Correlates of Meaning in Life from Emerging Adulthood to Older Adulthood," *Journal of Positive Psychology* 4, no. 1 (2009): 43–52.

8. Paul T. P. Wong, "Positive Psychology 2.0: Towards a Balanced Interactive Model of the Good Life," *Canadian Psychology* 52, no. 2 (2011): 69–81. See also Dr. Paul Wong, "What Is Second Wave Positive Psychology and Why Is It Necessary?" http://www.drpaul wong.com/what-is-second-wave-positive-psychology-and-why-is-it -necessary/.

9. See the Second International Congress on Cognitive Behavioral Coaching, in Athens, Greece, at which Dr. Alex Pattakos was a keynote speaker (http://www.iccbc2016.com/). Also, in 2015, Alex was a keynote speaker at the International Existential Coaching Congress in Bogotá, Colombia.

10. See Alex Pattakos and Elaine Dundon, "Discovering Meaning Through the Lens of Work," *Journal of Constructivist Psychology*, DOI: 10.1080/10720537.2015.1119084 (2016). In addition, the Global Meaning Institute offers, as meaning-centered measurement tools, MEANINGology® Life, MEANINGology® Work, and MEANINGology® Team & Organizations Tests.

11. Alex Pattakos, "The Search for Meaning in Government Service," *Public Administration Review* 64, no. 1 (2004): 106. See also Panagiotis Karkatsoulis, Alex Pattakos, and Efi Stefopoulou, "Looking for Ariadne's Thread: Greece's Public Service Workforce in Transition," *PA Times* 37, no. 2 (2014): 4–5.

12. Laurence E. Lynn, *Managing the Public's Business: The Job of the Government Executive* (New York: Basic Books, 1981).

13. "Viktor Frankl" entry in *New World Encyclopedia*, http://www.new worldencyclopedia.org/entry/Viktor_Frankl.

14. Mike Fleming Jr., "Holocaust Memoir 'Man's Search for Meaning' Heading to Screen," *Deadline*, June 8, 2015, online at http://deadline .com/2015/06/viktor-frankl-holocaust-memoir-mans-search-for -meaning-movie-1201439694/; see also Henry Barnes, "Viktor Frankl's Book on the Psychology of the Holocaust to Be Made

into a Film," June 9, 2015, online at http://www.theguardian.com/
film/2015/jun/09/viktor-frankls-book-on-the-psychology-of-the
-holocaust-to-be-made-into-a-film. In June 2016 it was reported that
another production company, Straight Up Films, had acquired the
rights to develop a movie based on Viktor Frankl's memoir, *Man's
Search for Meaning* (http://variety.com/2016/film/news/viktor-frankl
-mans-search-for-meaning-movie-1201804466/). As the details of
this film project unfold and the partners in the movie's development
become clear, one thing is certain: our friends Alexander Vesely
MA, director and grandson of Viktor Frankl, and Mary Cimiluca,
producer of Noetic Films, Inc., are actively involved in a Hollywood
film project featuring the life and work of Dr. Viktor Frankl in
authentic ways, never before told!

15. Jonathan Zalman, "In Intensive Care, Jimmy Fallon Read 'Man's
Search for Meaning': The Late-night Host Nearly Lost His Finger,
but He Found Zen via Viktor Frankl," July 14, 2015, online at http://
www.tabletmag.com/scroll/192232/in-intensive-care-jimmy-fallon
-read-mans-search-for-meaning.

16. Interview with Jimmy Fallon, *Esquire* (December 2015–January
2016), online at http://www.esquire.com/entertainment/tv/a39744/
jimmy-fallon-interview/.

17. "Jimmy Fallon Searched for the Meaning of Life while in the ICU
for 10 Days," *Relevant*, July 14, 2015, online at http://www.relevant
magazine.com/slices/jimmy-fallon-searched-meaning-life-while-icu
-10-days.

18. For the "Law of the Forgetting Curve," see Hermann Ebbinghaus,
Memory: A Contribution to Experimental Psychology (New York:
Dover, 1964). This classic work was originally published as *Über das
Gedächtnis* (Leipzig: Duncker and Humblot, 1885).

19. *Viktor & I: An Alexander Vesely Film*, produced by Mary Cimiluca,
CEO, Noetic Films, Inc., 2010 (http://www.viktorandimovie.com/).

20. See Viktor Frankl Museum, Vienna, at http://www.franklzentrum
.org/english/viktor-frankl-museum-vienna.html.

21. Frankl, *Man's Search for Meaning*, 134.

22. For more on the Statue of Responsibility, see http://www.statueof
responsibility.com/. See also Ken Shelton and Daniel Louis Bolz,
eds., *Responsibility 911: With Great Liberty Comes Great Responsibility*
(Provo, UT: Executive Excellence Publishing, 2008). Alex Pattakos,
"Life, Liberty, and the Pursuit of Meaning," in *Responsibility 911*,
72–75.

References

Aburdene, Patricia. 2005. *Megatrends 2010: The Rise of Conscious Capitalism*. Charlottesville, VA: Hampton Roads.

Albion, Mark. 2000. *Making a Life: Reclaiming Your Purpose and Passion in Business and in Life*. New York: Warner Books.

Bains, Gurnek, et al. 2007. *Meaning Inc.: The Blueprint for Business Success in the 21st Century*. London: Profile Books.

Batthyany, Alexander, and David Guttmann. 2005. *Empirical Research on Logotherapy and Meaning-Oriented Psychotherapy: An Annotated Bibliography*. Phoenix: Zeig, Tucker & Theisen.

Batthyany, Alexander, and Jay Levinson. 2009. *Existential Psychotherapy of Meaning*. Phoenix: Zeig, Tucker & Theisen.

Battino, Rubin. 2002. *Meaning: A Play Based on the Life of Viktor Frankl*. Williston, VT: Crown House.

Bulka, Reuven P. 1979. *The Quest for Ultimate Meaning: Principles and Applications of Logotherapy*. New York: Philosophical Library.

Coetzer, Patti Havenga. 2003. *Viktor Frankl's Avenues to Meaning: A Compendium of Concepts, Phrases, and Terms in Logotherapy*. Benmore: Viktor Frankl Foundation of South Africa.

Covey, Stephen R. 1989. *The 7 Habits of Highly Effective People*. New York: Simon & Schuster.

Covey, Stephen R., A. Roger Merrill, and Rebecca R. Merrill. 1994. *First Things First: To Live, to Love, to Learn, to Leave a Legacy*. New York: Simon & Schuster.

Dik, Bryan J., Zinta S. Byrne, and Michael F. Steger, eds. 2013. *Purpose and Meaning in the Workplace*. Washington, DC: American Psychological Association.

Dundon, Elaine. 2002. *The Seeds of Innovation: Cultivating the Synergy That Fosters New Ideas*. New York: AMACOM Books.

Ebbinghaus, Hermann. 1964. *Memory: A Contribution to Experimental Psychology*. New York: Dover.

Fabry, Joseph B. 1968. *The Pursuit of Meaning: Logotherapy Applied to Life*. Boston: Beacon.

———. 1988. *Guideposts to Meaning: Discovering What Really Matters*. Oakland, CA: New Harbinger.

Fabry, Joseph B., Reuven P. Bulka, and William S. Sahakian, eds. 1995. *Finding Meaning in Life: Logotherapy*. Northvale, NJ: Jason Aronson.

Frankl, Viktor E. 1967. *Psychotherapy and Existentialism*. New York: Simon & Schuster.

———. 1978. *The Unheard Cry for Meaning*. New York: Washington Square.

———. 1986. *The Doctor and the Soul: From Psychotherapy to Logotherapy*. New York: Vintage Books.

———. 1988. *The Will to Meaning: Foundations and Applications of Logotherapy*. New York: New American Library.

———. 1992. *Man's Search for Meaning*. 4th ed. Boston: Beacon.

———. 1997a. *Man's Search for Ultimate Meaning*. New York: Plenum.

———. 1997b. *Recollections: An Autobiography*. New York: Plenum.

Gill, Ajaipal Singh. 2000. *Frankl's Logotherapy and the Struggle Within*. Pittsburgh: Dorrance.

Gould, William Blair. 1993. *Frankl: Life with Meaning*. Pacific Grove, CA: Brooks/Cole.

Graber, Ann V. 2003. *Viktor Frankl's Logotherapy: Method of Choice in Ecumenical Pastoral Psychology*. Lima, OH: Wyndham Hall.

Guttmann, David. 2008. *Finding Meaning in Life, at Midlife and Beyond*. Westport, CT: Praeger.

Kimble, Melvin A. 2000. *Viktor Frankl's Contribution to Spirituality and Aging*. New York: Haworth.

Klingberg, Haddon. 2001. *When Life Calls Out to Us: The Love and Lifework of Viktor and Elly Frankl*. New York: Doubleday.

Lent, Timothy. 2004. *Viktor E. Frankl Anthology*. Bloomington, IN: Xlibris.

Lukas, Elisabeth. 1984. *Meaningful Living: A Logotherapy Guide to Health*. New York: Grove.

———. 1986. *Meaning in Suffering: Comfort in Crisis Through Logotherapy*. Berkeley: Institute of Logotherapy Press.

———. 2000. *Logotherapy Textbook*. Toronto: Liberty Press.

Martin, Mike. W. 2000. *Meaningful Work*. New York: Oxford University Press.

McCain, John. 1999. *Faith of My Fathers*. New York: Random House.

Morgan, John H. 1987. *From Freud to Frankl: Our Modern Search for Personal Meaning*. Bristol, IN: Wyndham Hall.

Naylor, Thomas H., William H. Willimon, and Magdaelena R. Naylor. 1994. *The Search for Meaning*. Nashville: Abingdon.

Pattakos, Alex, and Elaine Dundon. 2015. *The OPA! Way: Finding Joy & Meaning in Everyday Life & Work*. Dallas, TX: BenBella Books.

Redsand, Anna S. 2006. *Viktor Frankl: A Life Worth Living*. New York: Clarion Books.

Shelton, Ken, and Daniel Louis Bolz, eds. 2008. *Responsibility 911: With Great Liberty Comes Great Responsibility*. Provo, UT: Executive Excellence Publishing.

Taylor, Charles. 1991. *The Ethics of Authenticity*. Cambridge, MA: Harvard University Press.

Tengan, Andrew. 1999. *Search for Meaning as the Basic Human Motivation*. Frankfurt, Germany: Peter Lang.

Terez, Tom. 2000. *22 Keys to Creating a Meaningful Workplace*. Holbrook, MA: Adams Media.

Wong, Paul T. P., and Prem S. Fry, eds. 1998. *The Human Quest for Meaning*. Mahwah, NJ: Lawrence Erlbaum.

Acknowledgments

Writing a book is like growing a garden. One cannot expect to plant a seed and have a full-grown flower the next day. We could not have written this book without the support and patience of many people along the way. We are grateful for the support of the Frankl family, who believed in and supported this book from the beginning. Thank you to the entire team at Berrett-Koehler Publishers (especially publisher Steve Piersanti and Jeevan Sivasubramaniam, managing director–editorial, as well as the editors, reviewers, designers, operations staff, and all other B-K contributors and fellow authors) for seeking to create a world that works for all. Thank you to Janet Thomas. We would especially like to thank all of those who believed in and encouraged us to expand our meaning movement. The movement is catching on and we know, together, we can spread the meaning message around the world. The best is yet to come.

Index

International Journal of Individual Psychology, 15
International Journal of Psychoanalysis, 14
Intrinsic motivation, 175
Introspection. See Self-discovery

Jackson, Phil, 61–62
Jaeger, Andrea, 133
Janet (vignette), 101–102
Jesus, 230n4
Job descriptions, 186–187
Job titles, 186–187
Jobs, Steve, 63, 210
John, Saint, 230n4
Joshua (vignette), 146–147

Kabat-Zinn, Jon, 55–56
Kennedy, John F., 197
Kids' Stuff Foundation, 133

Labyrinth (of meaning)
in corporate world, 58–61
life as a, 57–61
Pattakos's personal journey, 57–58
work life as a, 103–104
Laing, R. D., xiv
Larry King Live, 29
Leadership, 184–185
Legacy
defined, 79–80
drafting our, 79–82
Legend of Bagger Vance, The (motion picture), 70
Levine, Stewart, 231n5
Life Is Beautiful (motion picture), 123
"Living the good life," 157
Logos, 15–16, 230n4
Logotherapy, xx, 15–21
as approach to discovering meaning, 214
changing lives, 214–216
first use of word, 15
and meaning as foundation of existence, 15
Pattakos as practitioner of, 2
self-transcendence and, 130–131
spiritual dimension of, 139–140

Viktor Frankl Institute and, 20–21, 217
Long, Jerry L., Jr., 215–216
Love, 78, 213
and corporate culture, 186

Malden Mills, 199–200
Management. See Academy of Management; Bosses; Corporate culture; MBWA (management by walking around)
Mandela, Nelson, 27–28, 134
Man's Search for Meaning (Frankl)
diplomat patient, 75–76
feature film of, 222
impact of, 56, 215
original subtitle, 20
on SS officer, 134
Manzoni, Jean-François, 94
Mark (vignette), 41–43
Maslow, Abraham, xii–xiii
Mass murder, 130
Mass neurotic triad, 54, 193, 210
Material possessions and inner emptiness, 54
Materialism, 77
Mayo Clinic, 181–182
MBWA (management by walking around), 94–95
McBurney, Ralph Waldo, 35–36
McCain, John, 19
Meaning. See also specific topics
crisis of, 8–9, 144–148, 154
definitions, 9–10, 77, 151
finding, xix
as foundation of existence, 15
greed and, 52
Meaning, will to, 50, 53, 143, 227. See also specific topics
centrality of, 55, 63
cry for meaning and, 53–55
at Malden Mills, 199–200
Meaning analysis, 148–150, 160
Meaning-centric leadership, 185
Meaning culture, 179. See also Culture: meaning-centered
The Meaning Difference®, 162f

About the Authors

Alex Pattakos, PhD, affectionately nicknamed "Dr. Meaning," is the cofounder of the Global Meaning Institute, with offices in the United States, Canada, and Greece. He is passionate about helping people realize their full potential by finding authentic meaning in their lives and work. His unique background includes being a former therapist and mental health administrator, a full-time professor of public and business administration, including graduate program head, a consultant with the White House under three presidents, and an adviser to the commissioner of the U.S. Food and Drug Administration. With his passion for exploring new and meaningful solutions to public issues, Alex was one of the initial faculty evaluators for the Innovations in American Government Awards Program at the John F. Kennedy School of Government, Harvard University. He is coauthor of the award-winning book *The OPA! Way: Finding Joy & Meaning in Everyday Life & Work*. Now as cofounder of the Global Meaning Institute and leader of the meaning movement, Alex is focused on advising, speaking, and teaching about MEANINGology® and how to bring meaning to life, work, and society.

Linda Carfagno Photography, Santa Fe

Elaine Dundon, MBA, is the cofounder of the Global Meaning Institute, with offices in the United States, Canada, and Greece. The Global Meaning Institute is establishing itself as a world leader in meaning through its leading-edge research, MEANINGology® Tests/ Assessments, education programs and materials, and strategic advising. She is passionate about helping people find meaning in their personal and work lives as well as helping organizations create meaning-centered workplaces to deliver products and services that truly make a meaningful difference. Elaine began her career in marketing strategy and brand management at Procter & Gamble. A thought leader in the field of personal and organizational innovation, she authored the international best-selling book *The Seeds of Innovation* and created the groundbreaking course on innovation management at the University of Toronto. Her work evolved to the "human side of innovation," incorporating meaning, leadership, philosophy, and metaphysics to help people and organizations reach their full potential. She is the coauthor of the award-winning book *The OPA! Way: Finding Joy & Meaning in Everyday Life & Work*. Now a cofounder of the Global Meaning Institute, Elaine is using her unique background to lead MEANINGology® and the meaning movement, encouraging all to live and work with meaning.

For further information:

Global Meaning Institute
email: info@globalmeaninginstitute.com
web: www.globalmeaninginstitute.com

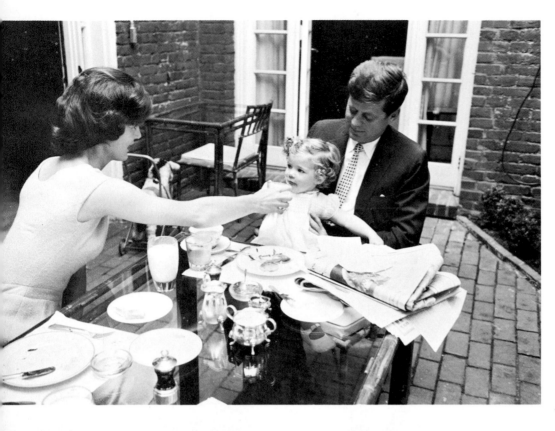

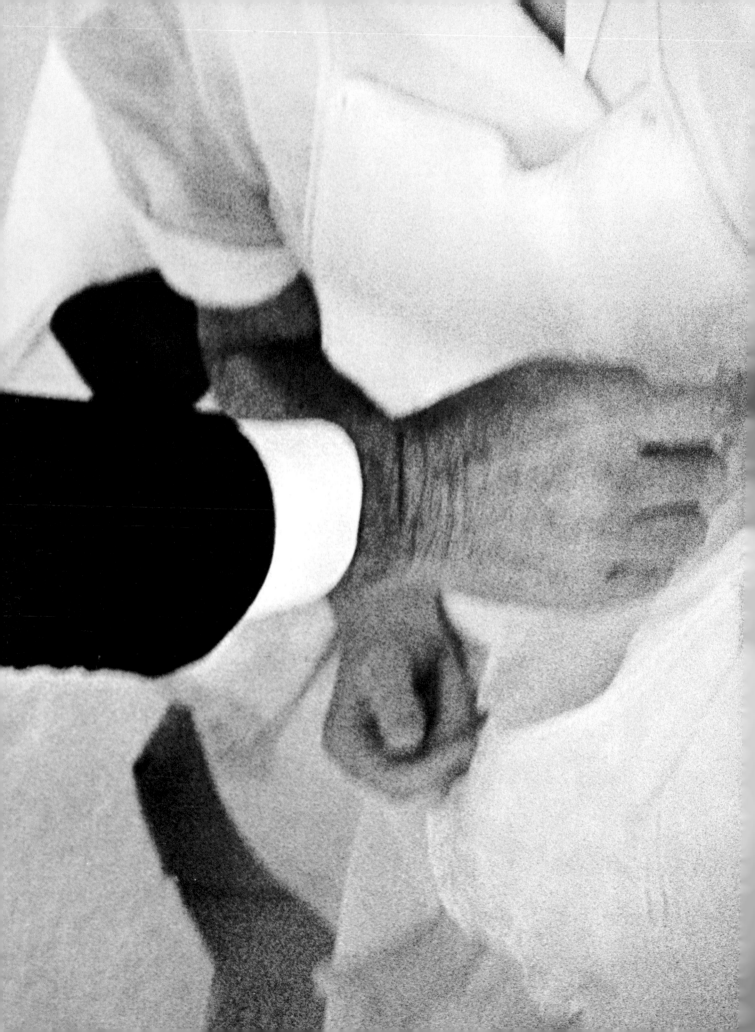

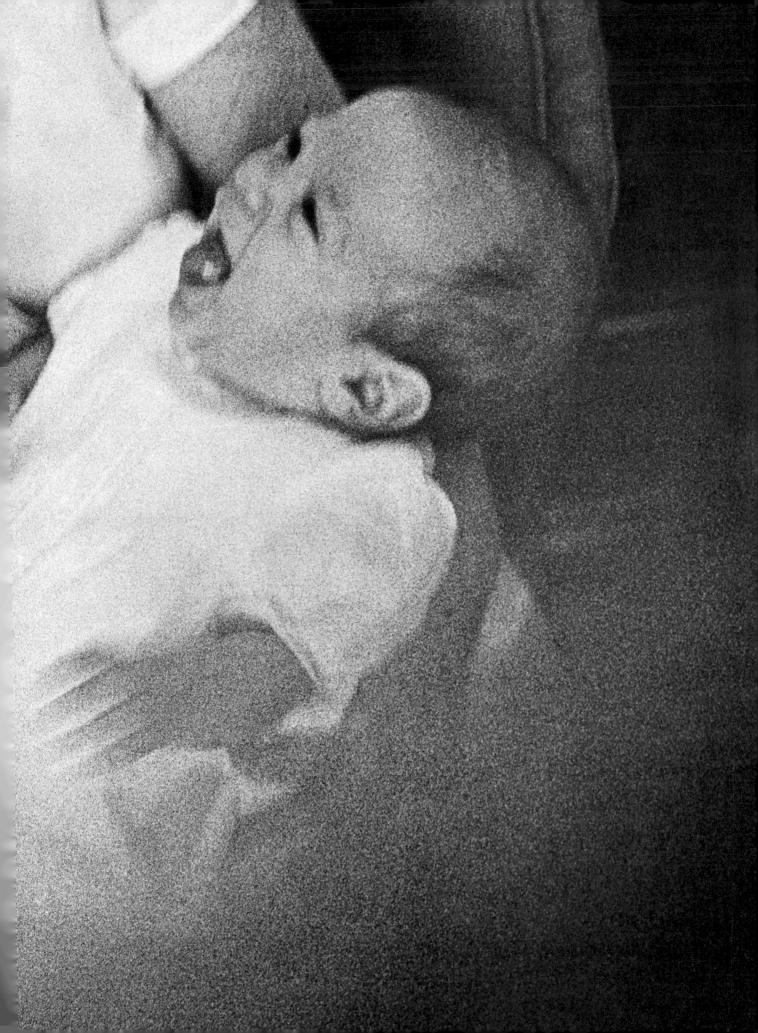

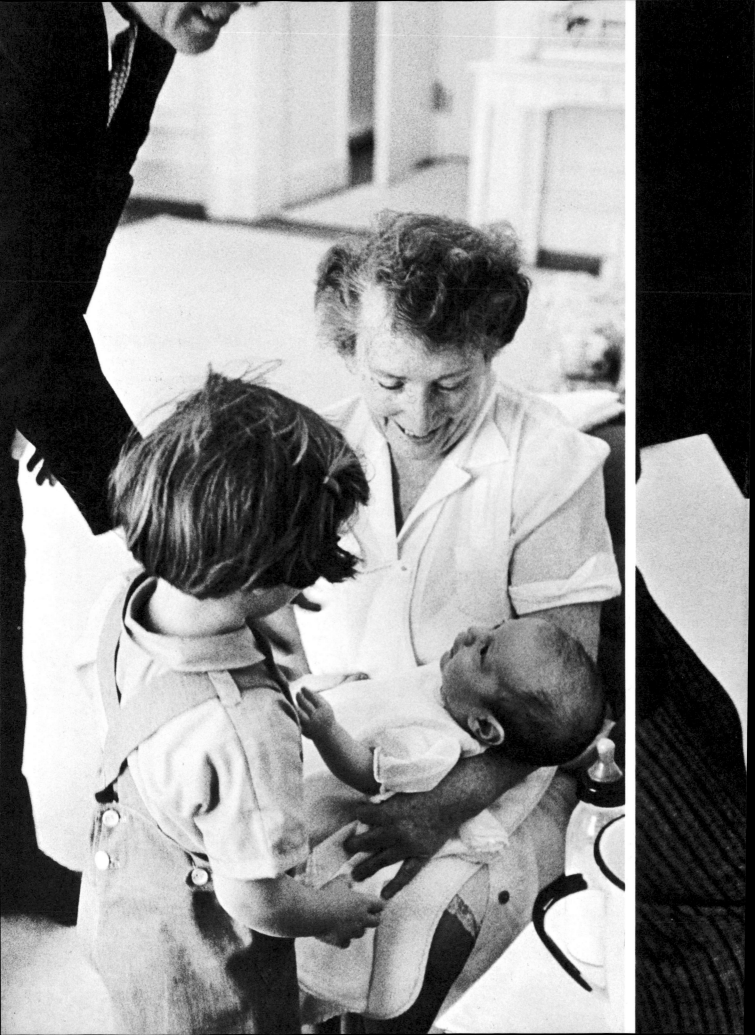

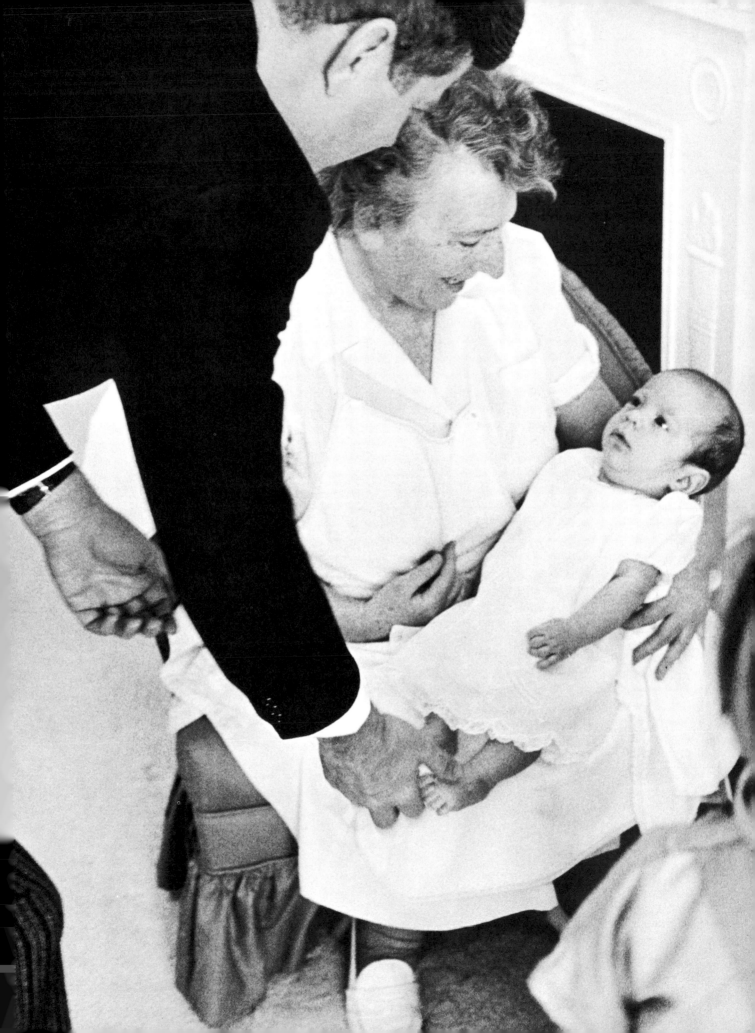

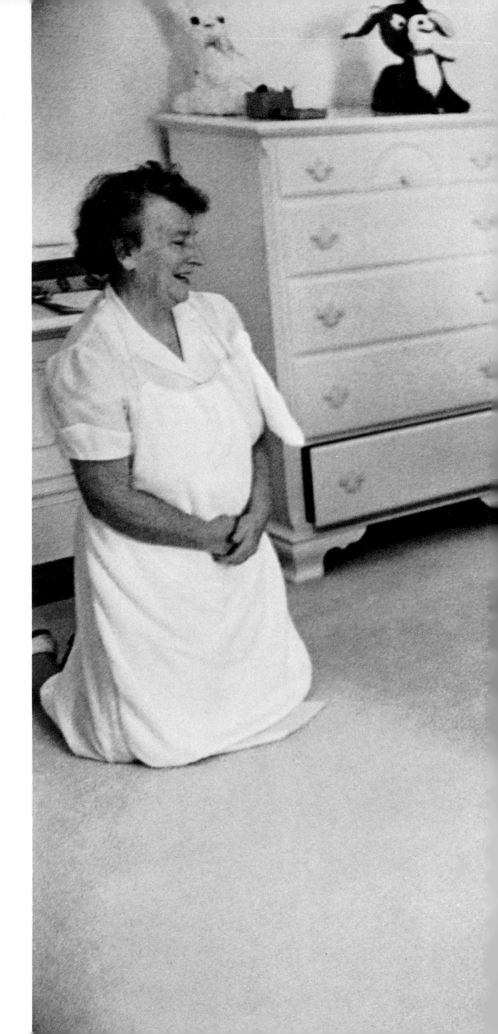

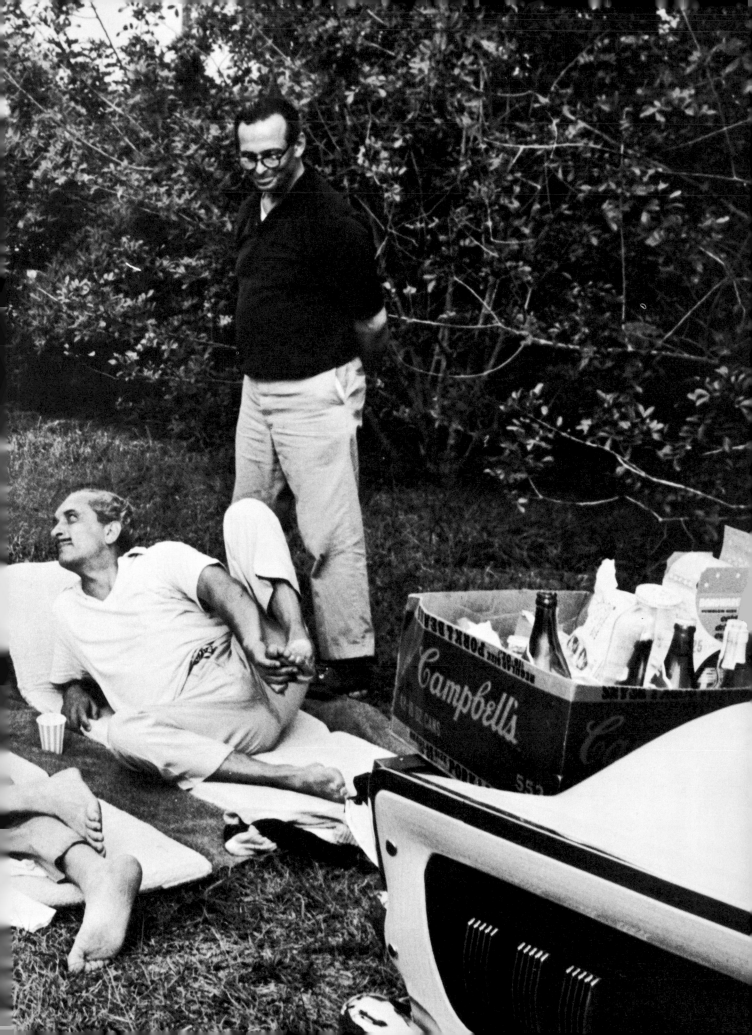

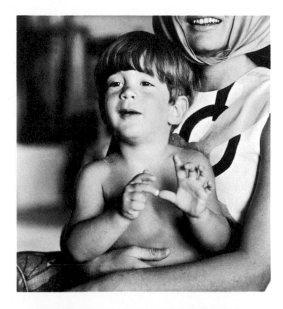

144

John Fitzgerald Kennedy
1917-1963

THIS BOOK IS DEDICATED TO MY FRIEND AND COMPANION
DR. MAX JACOBSON

ACKNOWLEDGMENTS

My deepest appreciation to:
Sam Sako, my faithful darkroom man, Trudy Owett, my personal
assistant, Clifford Wolf, my photographic assistant, and
the Studio personnel: R.O., D.W., M.B., M.O., V.H.

Robert Cato, who helped select the pictures and designed the book.

The editors of *Life,* who gave me the initial assignment to
photograph John F. Kennedy.

And most of all my wife Pat Suzuki, who through the years gave
me the encouragement and time to prepare this book.

Some of the photographs in this book have appeared in *Life,
Ladies' Home Journal, McCall's* and *Redbook.* The pictures on
pages 29, 52-53, 90 and 146-147 were first published in *Vogue.*

Notes on the Photographs in This Book

This book is not intended to be a complete photographic record or documentary of the John F. Kennedy family. The pictures are not in chronological order and I have avoided supplying specific dates, because with few exceptions the day or event was not important. For the most part these photographs are not of state occasions or ceremonies, nor do they show moments of crisis or violence. These photographs were taken in order to catch and reflect the mood, the feeling of a given moment. If the viewer receives from these pictures an understanding of the affection of the Kennedys for one another, their high spirits and enjoyment of life, the book will have fulfilled its purpose.

M.S.

Title page: Hyannis Port in the fall of the year. The children are Robert Kennedy's.

Opening page: An official picture, never used, taken at the time of the Bay of Pigs disaster. The President later commented that he had decided not to release it. "I looked too serious." It was a grim, tense day, but he brought none of this to the top floor of the White House. Afterward he had lunch, a sandwich and fruit on a small tray. He made no mention of the cause and reason for his quiet.

The sailing series: Taken off Hyannis Port in the fall. Sunny days and after a round of golf everyone raced to the end of the dock and went sailing. It was the practice that before the Kennedy children could sail, they would be thrown overboard in the open sea with life preservers so that they wouldn't panic when they later had an accidental plunge.

Next two double-page pictures: Late afternoon on the back lawn of Joseph Kennedy's house in Hyannis Port. One was always aware of the three family houses facing the tree-covered street. In front, leaves on the ground; in back, the gently rolling lawn down to the Atlantic Ocean. I was most conscious of the flow of children — the area was later aptly called the "Compound." Clothes were casual. A strong bent for the active life and also an intense life of reading, discussion of current events, and general awareness.

Strolling through the back of Robert Kennedy's house. Underneath, the children running and showering. Never the feeling of pressure or time.

Following page 21: Georgetown, the last weeks before election. Breakfast early but leisurely, time to read the paper and talk and play with the children. After J.F.K. left for the Senate Office Building, Jackie would stay around the house until later in the morning, when she usually took a walk by the Georgetown canal.

Dinner at Georgetown with Senator and Mrs. John Sherman Cooper. George the butler.

The Senate office, just before election.

Page 38 and following: Wheeling, West Virginia, a real pressure point. In the first picture are some of the people who surrounded Senator Kennedy in the early days of the campaign. It was an oppressive, one-hundred-degree day, uncomfortable as could be; a small town, glass-blowing and steel, and a typical campaign kind of circus. In the basement of a church the speech was given, and there was a cake in the shape of the White House. J.F.K. was in fine form, enjoying as always the people around him. He seemed to have boundless energy. This series, taken during a crucial campaign, went through as a blur of heat. All through this campaign there was the whirling on one side and the peaceful life in Georgetown on the other.

At the Virginia estate of Jacqueline Kennedy's mother, Mrs. Hugh D. Auchincloss.

Pages 55-61: Hyannis Port. The children growing up, surrounded by natural life, horses, sports, and travel.

Page 62: The twin-engine plane used for commuting between Boston and the Cape.

Pages 65-94: The John F. Kennedys at Hyannis Port. Typically the family was together, always celebrating birthdays, parties, anniversaries, conscious of outdoor life, the beach and the air. Most afternoons were spent along the water, walking, talking and playing with the children. Everyone would dress for dinner and gather in the living room. The talk would be on politics and the arts, and to be uninformed in that group was disaster. World history was attacked in the manner of an athletic contest. It was an adults' world after dark.

The inauguration gala started hours late because of the heavy snow. Less than half the guests were there at the beginning.

The White House nursery. The President, dressed to make a speech, stopped to play with John-John. Mrs. Maud Shaw, the proud nanny. Caroline, pleased to have her father there, kept playing around and finally the President scooped up John-John with a big hug and a little dance. Caroline thought of her brother as her personal doll. There was the same feeling as at Hyannis Port or Georgetown, except that this was the nursery on the top floor of the White House.

Page 104: Hyannis Port. Caroline being a photographer's assistant. John-John, his friend David Shaw, and Caroline all fighting over the buttered toast. The Kennedys start early to assert themselves.

Page 105 and following: The White House again. Caroline sneaking out from under the nursery bed to play with John-John and ending up taking my picture.

On the trampoline at Hyannis Port, full of enthusiasm and life.

The center hallway on the top floor of the White House, a sort of salon. At the far end was the Lincoln guest bedroom; the near end was used by the President and First Lady. On the left, a small private dining room.

The official photograph of John-John at one year, with Caroline and Jackie.

Caroline, the photographer's assistant, struggling to get John-John to stand. She carried the tripod and talked about my "yellow bird" airplane. She identified the plane with the photographs.

Pablo Casals. A most important night and Casals was like a small boy, happy and excited. There was a feverish air in the White House. When the concert was over and the President spoke, there was no other sound. It was a sparkling yet restrained evening. There was a small dinner for Casals and the musicians, who had not eaten before the performance, and everyone gathered around. The private dinner party lasted late into the evening.

Pages 130-133: The President's warning to a too-soft America to toughen up set off that craze, the fifty-mile walk. Everybody was doing it. After Robert Kennedy completed his speedy hike, the President's brother-in-law, Prince Radziwill, ended dinner one evening by saying he could do it. So began a test of physical and emotional determination. Agent Clint Hill, Charles (Chuck) Spalding, the President's roommate at Harvard, Stash Radziwill and others gaily started from quiet Palm Beach at one in the morning. It was typical of the enthusiasm for group projects. Friends loaded station wagons with steaks and fruit juice to follow the men down the Sunshine Parkway towards Miami.

All day the state troopers waved to the group, and tourists driving by looked over their shoulders in amazement.

Suddenly in the afternoon, without warning, the big white Lincoln rolled up, driven by the President. He had left his yacht to come and see how the group was faring. Various tender spots were displayed and Dr. Max Jacobson carefully checked the wounded extremities. He had been talked out of the hike after eleven miles when he turned his ankle. Stash was determined that the Polish banner would fly high, and Chuck that his Harvard class banner equally so.

Off and on during the day the First Lady, her sister Lee and agent Paul Landis brought some cheer to the weary hikers. By late afternoon, however, the gayness had worn off and a grim, determined group raced to try to keep up with Bob Kennedy's record time. The President was worried about Stash,

but Dr. Max was on hand. It was difficult to keep Dr. Max from competing; as always, he was everybody's "good friend," and insisted on treating everyone in sight.

When darkness fell and the fifty miles were finally ours, all gathered at the Palm Beach White House for champagne and the President's "decorations"; inscribed tea bags in place of medals.

Page 134 and following: Palm Beach, the time of the announcement of the impending arrival of a third child. The dog Clipper playing in the water, John-John back of the house by the pool. John-John with a sense of humor and a twinkle in his eye. These were warm, happy times, with no feeling of the pressures that were to come.

Hyannis Port.

The President's office, November, 1963.

All of the photographs in this book, with the exception of the Casals series, were taken with a Nikon camera and Nikor lenses.

THE
JOHN F. KENNEDYS

BY

MARK SHAW

DESIGNED BY ROBERT CATO

THE
JOHN F. KENNEDYS

BY

MARK SHAW

A FAMILY ALBUM

FARRAR, STRAUS

Berrett–Koehler
Publishers

Connecting people and ideas
to create a world that works for all

Dear Reader,

Thank you for picking up this book and joining our worldwide community of Berrett-Koehler readers. We share ideas that bring positive change into people's lives, organizations, and society.

To welcome you, we'd like to offer you a free e-book. You can pick from among twelve of our bestselling books by entering the promotional code **BKP92E** here: http://www.bkconnection.com/welcome.

When you claim your free e-book, we'll also send you a copy of our e-newsletter, the *BK Communiqué*. Although you're free to unsubscribe, there are many benefits to sticking around. In every issue of our newsletter you'll find

- A free e-book
- Tips from famous authors
- Discounts on spotlight titles
- Hilarious insider publishing news
- A chance to win a prize for answering a riddle

Best of all, our readers tell us, "Your newsletter is the only one I actually read." So claim your gift today, and please stay in touch!

Sincerely,

Charlotte Ashlock
Steward of the BK Website

Questions? Comments? Contact me at bkcommunity@bkpub.com.

Certified Sourcing
www.sfiprogram.org
SFI-00453

Certified

Corporation
bcorporation.net

Berrett–Koehler
BK Publishers

Berrett-Koehler is an independent publisher dedicated to an ambitious mission: *connecting people and ideas to create a world that works for all.*

We believe that to truly create a better world, action is needed at all levels—individual, organizational, and societal. At the individual level, our publications help people align their lives with their values and with their aspirations for a better world. At the organizational level, our publications promote progressive leadership and management practices, socially responsible approaches to business, and humane and effective organizations. At the societal level, our publications advance social and economic justice, shared prosperity, sustainability, and new solutions to national and global issues.

A major theme of our publications is "Opening Up New Space." Berrett-Koehler titles challenge conventional thinking, introduce new ideas, and foster positive change. Their common quest is changing the underlying beliefs, mindsets, institutions, and structures that keep generating the same cycles of problems, no matter who our leaders are or what improvement programs we adopt.

We strive to practice what we preach—to operate our publishing company in line with the ideas in our books. At the core of our approach is stewardship, which we define as a deep sense of responsibility to administer the company for the benefit of all of our "stakeholder" groups: authors, customers, employees, investors, service providers, and the communities and environment around us.

We are grateful to the thousands of readers, authors, and other friends of the company who consider themselves to be part of the "BK Community." We hope that you, too, will join us in our mission.

A BK Life Book

This book is part of our BK Life series. BK Life books change people's lives. They help individuals improve their lives in ways that are beneficial for the families, organizations, communities, nations, and world in which they live and work. To find out more, visit **www.bk-life.com**.